BSA BANTAM

Jeff Clew

CONTENTS

FOREWORD 4

HISTORY 5

EVOLUTION 10

SPECIFICATION 12

ROAD TESTS 17

OWNER'S VIEW 25

BUYING 29

CLUBS SPECIALISTS & BOOKS 31

PHOTO GALLERY 32

Foulis

Haynes

Titles in the *Super Profile* series

BSA Bantam (F333)
MV Agusta America (F334)
Norton Commando (F335)

Austin-Healey 'Frogeye' Sprite (F343)
Ferrari 250GTO (F308)
Ford GT40 (F332)
Jaguar D-Type & XKSS (F371)
Jaguar Mk 2 Saloons (F307)
Lotus Elan (F330)
MGB (F305)
Morris Minor & 1000 (ohv) (F331)
Porsche 911 Carrera (F311)

Further titles in this series will be published at
regular intervals. For information on new titles
please contact your bookseller or write to the
publisher.

ISBN 0 85429 333 7

A FOULIS Motorcycling Book

First published 1983

Published by:
Haynes Publishing Group
Sparkford, Yeovil,
Somerset BA22 7JJ

Distributed in USA by:
Haynes Publications Inc.
861 Lawrence Drive, Newbury
Park, California 91320, USA

Editor: Rod Grainger
Dust jacket design: Rowland Smith
Page Layout: Teresa Woodside
Colour photography: Andrew Morland
Road tests: Courtesy of *Motor Cycling*
and *Motor Cycle* (IPC)
Printed in England by: J.H.Haynes &
Co. Ltd

FOREWORD

I am especially pleased to have the opportunity of writing this first motorcycle title in the Foulis *Super Profile* series. Although the BSA Bantam may be regarded by some as one of the 'grey porridge' machines of the immediate postwar era, it had a certain charm all its own ... if only because it brought low cost motorcycling within the realm of many who otherwise might never have taken to a powered two-wheeler as a means of transportation. Countless learners cut their teeth on the humble Bantam, which was easy to maintain and remarkably free from vices if it was looked after with reasonable care. It formed the backbone of many RAC/ACU Training Schemes and was used extensively by the GPO telegram delivery boys. In racing it earned respect by putting up some quite remarkable performances in the Isle of Man as well as other speed venues. In trials it made its mark too, even in some of the classic events.

The only Bantam I have owned was a 1955 plunger suspension D3 model, which I acquired in the form of a collection of rusty and well-worn bits in 'kit' form. Its conversion into a very usable trials model was an experience I enjoyed, and I was glad that I had derived much useful knowledge from my earlier authorship of the *BSA Bantam Owners Workshop Manual*, which happened to be the second title I tackled when I started up the Haynes motorcycle workshop manual project late in 1972. This title spanned the complete Bantam production run and helped stimulate my appreciation of a design that started life in Germany. I have often wondered how much of the market the Bantam stole from the LE Velocette, for although the latter should have been on the market first, representing the ultimate in the 'everyman' concept, irritating pre-production problems delayed its release until just after the Bantam had made its debut. Although the LE was a much more sophisticated design, it carried a much higher price tag too. At that time, a new, lower-priced utility model would have had the advantage in capturing the lower end of the market, and I suspect BSA made the most of the opportunity that unwittingly came their way. With these facts in mind, I needed little encouragement to pay tribute to the Bantam by recording this, its life history.

I would like to acknowledge, with grateful thanks, the assistance of Bantam expert and fellow author Roy Bacon in reading through the manuscript and offering his criticism and advice. My thanks go also to my good friend Harry Sucher for permitting me to use some of the material about the Hummer and Ranger variants from his definitive history of Harley-Davidson entitled *Harley-Davidson: The Milwaukee Marvel*

H.6942

(Haynes/Foulis). Mick Woollett, the Editor-in-Chief of *Motor Cycle Weekly*, kindly gave permission for the reproduction of some of the original road tests published in *Motor Cycling* and *Motor Cycle* during the period covered. Ted Fithian and Erwin Tragatsch helped out with some of the more unusual and difficult to obtain photographs, whilst Roy Bacon and Martin Baldwin covered Bantam racing and also lent me some useful photographs. Cyril Halliburn kindly produced some BSA factory photographs from his archives, and my good friend Cyril Ayton, editor of *Motorcycle Sport*, helped fill in some of the gaps from photographs in his possession. Thanks are also due to VEB Motorradwerk Zschopau for supplying photographs of the DKW RT125.

The photographs showing model differences and close-ups of various components were taken by Andrew Morland and I am particularly grateful to John Eyles, Dave Jenkin and Pete Dungey for making their machines so readily available for the photographic sessions. John Eyles also responded to my request for an interview, as did Timothy Nichol and Brian Ing. All can be regarded as true Bantam enthusiasts and this book is the richer for their help.

Jeff Clew

HISTORY

A False Start

It was not until 1927 that BSA Cycles Limited, as they were then known, showed any interest in two-stroke motorcycles. Until then, all of their designs had used a four-stroke engine, even the lightweight models such as their famous round tank design. But times were changing and with the gathering gloom that preceded the economic depression that was soon to become only too evident, most manufacturers had an eye on utility machines that would cater for the lower end of the market. Obviously a two-stroke design had certain advantages in manufacturing economics, which would permit a relatively low retail price yet show a reasonable profit margin. With these factors in mind, and the prospect of mass sales, one may presume this is why BSA opted for a two-stroke.

The new two-stroke machine made its debut at the 1927 Olympia Show and was seen to embody quite a number of unusual features, not the least of which was a kickstarter on the nearside. Of 174cc capacity, the engine had bore and stroke dimensions of 60 x 61.5mm and was built in-unit with a two-speed, hand-change gearbox. A large diameter exposed flywheel was attached to the left-hand side of the crankshaft, with the carburettor immediately behind it, the intake being just above the top of the flywheel rim. Ignition was by means of a magneto mounted immediately behind the cylinder, and lubrication was by the time-honoured petroil system. A decompressor was fitted to the cylinder head and the exhaust system comprised a short down pipe to a circular expansion chamber mounted transversely in front of the crankcase. It vented via a short tailpipe with a small fishtail end. The cylinder head and barrel were a single casting, in cast iron.

The frame was of the pin-jointed type, in which nearly every tube was duplicated. Of conventional girder construction, the front forks had a central spring, but no provision for damping fork movement. Wheels were of 24 inch diameter, and each was fitted with a tyre of $2\frac{3}{8}$ inch section. The front wheel had no brake, two sets of brake shoes being fitted to the hub brake in the rear wheel and operated independently of each other by the customary handlebar lever and by a foot pedal on the left-hand side. This dual braking arrangement was necessary to meet legislation relating to motorcycle brakes at that time. Lighting was by dry battery on the model exhibited; the batteries being housed in a circular container clamped to the front down tube. A leather toolbox occupied the space between the rear of the saddle tube and the rear mudguard.

Appearance-wise, the newcomer was not particularly attractive, despite having the familiar green petrol tank with cream panels mounted at a rakish angle. More important, and as yet unknown to the public, the machine had only a mediocre performance, even in an era when the average two-stroke never rated very highly in the performance stakes. As a result, this first BSA two-stroke venture proved a dismal failure, which will explain why only three or four of these models have survived. Priced at £28.10s, the anticipated high volume sales were not realised, and when the two-stroke reappeared at the 1928 Olympia Show, several modifications had been deemed necessary.

Whilst the improved machine still adhered closely to the original's specification, the flywheel was now completely enclosed within a dished metal cover, similar in many respects to that fitted to contemporary Villiers engines. The carburettor now had an air cleaner that was fitted at a right-angle to the carburettor intake and pointed upwards so that it ran parallel to the front downtube of the frame. Of the two machines on display at the Show, one had a two-speed gearbox and the other a three-speed, the respective prices being £26.5s and £28. Other options included a front wheel fitted with a hub brake of $5\frac{1}{2}$ inches diameter (£1.1s extra), this option having become available soon after the original launch of the two-stroke. 'Proper' electric lighting cost an extra £5.10s, the magneto being replaced by a combined magneto and generator of the 'Maglita' type. Yet even these changes and options were not sufficient to make prospective buyers give the BSA two-stroke serious consideration. And so it was quietly withdrawn from the BSA catalogue, permitting the company once more to concentrate fully on its four-stroke designs. Almost 21 years were to pass before another two-stroke design was projected – discounting the moped of the late thirties that never went into production – fortunately, this would prove to be a much more successful venture ...

Birth of the 'Bantam'

News of another BSA two-stroke model came towards the end of February 1948, with an announcement in the motorcycling press related to an export order from Sweden. In this instance the engine capacity was only 123cc, some similarity to the earlier design being retained by the fact that this engine too was to be constructed on the unit-construction principle. But there the similarity ended, for this new design embodied all the latest innovations in contemporary two-stroke technology, including loop scavenging and the use of a deflectorless piston. It was emphasised that the manufacture of an engine/gear unit only, and not a complete machine, was envisaged. But as events subsequently showed, this decision was soon to be changed.

Having an exceptionally clean outward appearance, the engine unit's general attractiveness was enhanced by a slight forward inclination of the cylinder. The capacity of 123cc was achieved by bore and stroke measurements of 52 x 58mm. The piston had a slightly domed crown and was of low expansion alloy. It carried two pegged compression rings of 0.093 inch width. The skirt was cut away at each side to align with two transfer ports set opposite each other at 180°, the single exhaust port being set at right angles to them. The cylinder head was detachable, with a rear-mounted 14mm sparking plug, and with 13 vertical, tapering fins. It was cast in aluminium alloy and retained by four long studs that extended right through the cast iron cylinder barrel into the crankcase. The cylinder barrel had ten deep pitch fins and an additional two fins were cast into the top of the crankcase castings to provide extra rigidity. Two pinch bolts passed through the front and rear of the crankcase castings at this point. One of the early BSA instruction manuals implied that some models had a cast iron cylinder head, but presumably this is the result of some ambiguity as there is no evidence of Bantam heads ever having been cast in this material.

A full flywheel assembly was used, in conjunction with an 'I'

section connecting rod having an uncaged roller bearing big end and a phosphor bronze bush small end. The flywheels had cover plates forced into spigots machined in their outer faces, and were peened over to retain them in place. This arrangement increased crankcase compression, obviating the need for stuffers, although the plates had slots cut in them. The engine sprocket was attached to the right-hand end of the crankshaft assembly, a somewhat unusual arrangement in British motorcycle engineering. This necessitated having the primary drive and clutch on the right-hand side too. A Wico-Pacy generator was mounted on the left-hand end on the crankshaft assembly, the rotor being retained on a keyed taper. A ball race in each crankcase half, supported the crankshaft assembly, two on the drive side, using oil and compression seals of the garter type. A $\frac{5}{8}$ inch diameter Amal 261 carburettor looked after the mixture strength and was fitted with an air cleaner complete with shutter-type strangler to assist cold starting. Lubrication was by petroil, there being no provision for an oil pump.

The gearbox was housed within a separate compartment that formed part of the main crankcase castings. It was of the constant mesh three-speed type. Gear engagement was effected by means of dogs on the faces of the gear pinions and by splines on both the mainshaft and the layshaft. The positive stop selector mechanism utilised a claw fitted directly to the gearchange shaft, the pedal shaft and lever being returned to their original position after a gear had been selected. A ball bearing detent retained the gear selected in its correct location. An extension permitted the selector lever to give a visual indication of the gear selected by means of a pointer above the left-hand crankcase casting. Another somewhat unusual feature was the sharing of a common axis by the kickstarter and gearchange levers.

The clutch had three plates with cork inserts, interposed between the clutch housing-cum-chainwheel, two plain driving plates and a pressure plate with steel thimbles holding the six clutch springs. The pressure plate was retained by a large diameter circlip that located in a groove machined within the clutch housing and a recess in the pressure plate. Clutch operation was effected by a three-start worm to which the operating lever was attached. It pushed the two-piece pushrod through the hollow mainshaft, to separate the plates as it abutted on a hardened end piece in the centre of the pressure plate. An external screw-type adjuster was provided at the lever end, to make adjustment easy. The oil content of the gearbox was shared by the primary drive assembly, a combined filler and dipstick being found in the upper face of the right-hand crankcase casting, close to the carburettor. The oil capacity was approximately $\frac{3}{4}$ pint. Overall gear ratios from crankshaft to final drive were 7.05, 3.76 and 2.24:1. The complete engine/gear unit weighed about 45lbs.

It may seem strange that BSA should have come up with such an advanced design after showing so little interest in two-stroke engines. What the press release failed to mention was that the new machine was virtually a copy of the DKW RT125 engine unit that had been built at the Zschopauer Motorradwerk in Saxony, later to become the home of MZ when the initials were reversed. The design had been acquired by the Allied forces as a result of war reparations, and BSA had shown interest by making what amounted to a 'Chinese copy' in which they had rearranged the components in mirror fashion to have the kickstarter and gearchange lever on the right. At the same time, they also seized the opportunity to convert from metric to imperial dimensions, as an aid to manufacture in Birmingham. Even so, BSA had made an astute move, for, unlike its predecessor of 1927, the 1948 two-stroke was destined to become an unparalleled success.

As may be expected, the temptation to manufacture a complete motorcycle as opposed to just an engine unit proved overwhelming to a company with such excellent production facilities. During June 1948 the BSA model D1 was announced, initially labelled 'For Export Only'. When eventually it became available to home market purchasers during October, it retailed at a basic price of only £60, Purchase Tax increasing this to £74.4s, exclusive of the obligatory speedometer. At that time a speedometer was still regarded as an 'extra', even though it was a legal requirement!

At the official launch held towards the end of June, a somewhat low key affair due to the home market embargo, it was seen that the engine unit had been fitted into a frame and cycle parts of BSA design. The frame was of the single loop type and of all welded construction, the engine being retained by four bolts using small front and rear engine plates welded to the front downtube and the vertical saddle tube, respectively. Front suspension was by means of undamped telescopic forks, having helical springs screwed on to scrolls formed on the upper ends of the fork sliders and on an extension of the fork cap nuts. The top fork yoke was a simple pressing and the lower yoke a forging, the latter retaining the fork cover tubes by pinch bolts. The sliders were ground and then chromium plated to provide a good, hard wearing surface. They were supported by two widely-spaced sintered bronze bushes in each fork leg, the space between being filled with grease. A grease nipple fitted to the lower end of each cover tube facilitated lubrication at regular intervals, the gap between the sliders and the cover tubes being unsealed on the original design. The handlebars were fitted to the upper fork yoke

by split clamps, in front of which was mounted a 'D' shaped Smiths Chronometric speedometer of the non-trip type, calibrated up to 55mph. Drive came from the rear hub, which was slotted to engage with a spindle-mounted gearbox. The steering head bearings were of the cup and cone type, with provision for adjustment.

Deeply valanced mudguards were fitted, the front mudguard being rigidly mounted by means of stays and clips to the inside of each fork leg. The valances had a black panel to serve as the front number plate, and being of sufficiently deep section, there was adequate room for full front wheel movement. As the frame had a rigid rear end, the rear mudguard had a valance deeper at the front than at the rear. It had a carrier mounted on the top, to which the vertical stays were attached.

The front and rear wheels each had a hub brake of 5 inch diameter, with a width of $\frac{5}{8}$ inch. The front brake plate carried an outward facing lip with a recess that located around the right-hand fork slider, thus providing a suitable anchor point. It also formed a convenient mounting for the front brake cable adjuster. A heavyweight cable was employed, to obviate the risk of compression of the outer cover and a spongy brake action. The rear brake was rod operated via a foot pedal, and incorporated an adjuster at its furthermost end. The brake plate located with a peg welded to the inside of the frame, which prevented it from rotating. In both cases the brake shoes were diecast in aluminium and had steel facings at the point where the operating cam abutted.

The petrol tank was finished in pastel green, like the rest of the machine, and had a cream coloured panel on each side, with a surrounding gold line, which carried a winged BSA motif in maroon. Of $1\frac{7}{8}$ gallons capacity it was mounted by means of lugs at the front and rear that located with the steering

head and the front saddle mounting lug, respectively. The filler cap had an integral measure, three full measures of oil per gallon of petrol being the recommended mixing ratio, as also denoted on the top of the cap. The saddle was of the mattress type, with two rear springs and a three-point fixing. A rounded oblong-shaped toolbox, its lid retained by two coin-operated Dzus fasteners, was mounted on the right-hand side of the machine, by means of lugs welded to the top and bottom. It was located immediately below the saddle and carried the characteristic BSA piled arms motif on its lid.

The previously-mentioned Wico-Pacy generator supplied the ignition, access to the contact breaker being via a small diameter circular cover in the left-hand crankcase cover, retained by a pivoting strap. The generator also supplied the headlamp via separate lighting coils, the headlamp being supported by a separate bracket that bolted to the lower fork yoke.

A novel feature of the headlamp assembly was the remote control of the switch by means of a lever mounted on the handlebars. This actuated the switch by Bowden cable and resembled an air or ignition control in appearance. Four operating positions were provided: 'Off', 'Full', 'Dip' and 'Park'. The switch within the headlamp shell was of the spring-loaded, multi-contact type, the remote control making it much easier for the rider to operate the lights without need to reach over or around the speedometer – a sometimes difficult operation when the headlamp is low mounted and the switch is in the back of the shell. As there was no battery included in the circuit, lighting was available only when the engine was running. So that the machine could be parked with the lights on, there was provision within the headlamp shell for a replaceable dry battery. Because the electrical system was so basic, a bulb horn had to be fitted to satisfy legal requirements.

Conveniently, this was located through the centre of the steering head assembly, in the position normally occupied by the steering damper of a larger capacity machine.

As mentioned previously, carburation was by a small Amal carburettor with air cleaner and strangler. The exhaust pipe curved under the right-hand crankcase cover and terminated in a flat fishtail-type silencer that contained a semi-spiral baffle arrangement. Effective in action, it became one of the characteristic recognition features of the early models.

Final gear ratios were 7.0, 11.7 and 22.0:1. The machine had a 50in. wheelbase, a saddle height of 26in, a 5½in ground clearance, an overall height of 37in and an overall width of 28in. The weight was approximately 150lb.

Despite the enforced tone down of the initial launch, the representative from *Motor Cycling* managed to get in a 50-mile run and was able to report that the machine was outstandingly lively for one of such small capacity. He found he could cruise comfortably within the 40-45mph range and was able to achieve a maximum speed of just over 50mph. General comfort was good, despite the undamped forks and the rigid frame. The brakes in particular were commented upon as 'providing an exceptionally high degree of efficiency'. Sadly, the general public had to wait for at least another three months before they could form their own opinion, although a road test published during late October in the same magazine helped provide more details. By now the D1 had become known as the 'Bantam' and many were delighted to see petroil consumption had averaged out at 118mpg.

That the Bantam achieved almost instant popularity is now motorcycling history and it was no coincidence that by February 1957 150,000 had been sold. Yet surprisingly, it was not only as a cheap, reliable utility machine that Bantam had achieved such fame. 125cc racing was beginning to take a hold and in Australia in particular, where many of the early export models went, amateur engine tuners were obtaining quite remarkable results. Such were the increased centrifugal forces that resulted from their drastically modified Bantam engines that it was by no means unknown for the generator rotors to burst! Some Bantams appeared in British grass track races, the 125cc class usually being contested by sleeved down 150cc Royal Enfields and New Imperials. Although outclassed initially, it was not long before the Bantam began to offer serious challenge in this and the road racing sphere too. Soon, special proprietary parts became available with which to boost performance, such as special high compression cylinder heads, close ratio gears and special exhaust systems.

Trials riders saw prospects for the Bantam too, and three modified D1 models were entered for that classic of all trials, the 1949 Scottish Six Days. Later, the Post Office saw the Bantam as an ideal mount for their telegram delivery boys, and placed a substantial order. Finished in Post Office red, and with the Royal cypher on the petrol tank, they became a familiar sight on Britain's roads.

In America, Harley-Davidson had also taken up the war reparations option on the DKW RT125 design, making what was virtually an identical copy right down to the girder forks fitted with rubber band suspension. Marketed as the 'Hummer', the new model was unveiled at a Dealer Convention in Milwaukee on 24th November 1947, this launch preceding that of the British model. Despite the traditional allegiance to the large capacity vee twin, something like 10,000 Hummer models (123cc capacity) were sold during the first year of manufacture. By the time the 1949 Earls Court Show had opened, the D1 model had become available in a number of different guises, depending on the options selected. For example, an extra £6 would secure a machine fitted with Lucas rectified current lighting, the system having a 5 amp hour battery and a generator of Lucas manufacture in place of the original Wico-Pacy unit. Coil ignition was provided, too. For the expenditure of £5, a plunger-type spring frame could be supplied as part of the basic specification. Undamped, and providing only limited movement, it was none the less an improvement over the rigid frame version, albeit at the expense of a little extra weight. To these prices one had, of course, to add the ubiquitous Purchase Tax.

Also on display at the Show was a special competition version: evidence that the company had seen how well the Bantam lent itself to motorcycle sport. Similar in many respects to the rigid frame D1, the competition model differed in having a raised saddle, an upswept silencer, different footrests and a larger diameter rear wheel sprocket to effect a satisfactory reduction in the overall gear ratios. The tyre sections were changed too, that of the front tyre being 2.75in and the rear tyre 3.25in. It was around this time that the tank transfer was changed to the more familiar and colourful Bantam cockerel design.

There followed a continuous programme of development all the time the Bantam remained in production. Briefly, the 148cc version, catalogued as the D3 or Bantam Major model, appeared during 1954. Initially it too featured plunger-type rear suspension, but this was superseded by swinging arm rear suspension in 1956. The cylinder head and barrel had more generous finning and the original type of silencer was replaced by one of the torpedo type, which contained provision for removing the internal baffle assembly so that it could be cleaned more easily. A dualseat replaced the original saddle. A competition version of the D3 model was also available, but this was dropped from the range in conjunction with the original 123cc version when the swinging arm D3 came on the market. Although the trials two-stroke had already started to make its impact amongst trials riders, most were in favour of a machine fitted with at least a 197cc engine.

During 1958, the engine capacity was increased again, this time to 174cc for the introduction of the Bantam Super or D5 model. It subsequently evolved into the D7 model of similar capacity, as the result of the continuing development programme. The D10 appeared during 1966, also of 174cc capacity and was the first production model to have the option of a three or a four-speed gearbox. The D14 followed a year later. The only remaining model to be made in substantial numbers was the D14/4, which was alleged to develop 14bhp – ample evidence of the development work that had been going on behind the scenes.

Although the competition models had been dropped from the range during 1956, this did not mark the disappearance for all time of an off-road version. In 1966 what amounted to a trail bike version of the standard D10 model was listed as the 'Bushman'. Like its predecessors it featured an upswept exhaust system (which on this machine included the exhaust pipe too), lowered gear ratios, and more suitable tyres of the appropriate section. A crankcase undershield was included in the specification too. These machines had great potential amongst sheep farmers in Australia, but sadly BSA politics did not permit further modification to make the Bushman even more suitable for trials riding. The fact that Dave Rowland had taken second place to Sammy Miller in the 1967 Scottish Six Days Trial on a much modified Bushman was conveniently overlooked.

In America the capacity of the original Hummer version had been raised during 1953 to 165cc, whilst at the same time girder forks were replaced by a more modern telescopic design. Renamed the 'Ranger', production eventually came to a close during 1962, in favour of a new 175cc two-stroke, although an off-road trail bike version without lighting equipment lingered on for a while as the Super 10.

It was perhaps in road racing that the Bantam left its greatest legacy, for the activities of the Hogan brothers, George Todd, Fred Launchbury and others led to the eventual formation of the Bantam Racing Club during 1960. By laying down a detailed specification to which all eligible machines must conform, the Club prevented the possibility of 'freak' variants being evolved, so that Bantam enthusiasts had a cheap and convenient form of racing which extended even to entries in the Isle of Man TT. The Club still exists today and has already celebrated its 21st Anniversary.

One Bantam that has achieved immortality in a book is 'Oppy' – an early 123cc D1 model with the registration number OPE 811. Purchased by Peggy Iris Thomas it was used to convey her on a 14,000 mile journey through Canada, the United States and Mexico, with her dog Matelot seated on the rear carrier. Her adventures were recorded in the long out-of-print book entitled *A Ride in the Sun*, which was

published by Hodder and Stoughton during 1954. Strangely, the book has not a single illustration of rider or machine!

Production of the Bantam finally came to an end in March 1971, with the D175 model, of which comparatively few were made. Available in both standard and Bushman forms, the first of these models had appeared during 1969, having a new cylinder head with a centrally-located sparking plug, new crankcase castings and heavier front forks, to name but three changes in specification. Another version was on the stocks which featured a separate oil pump, according to Bert Hopwood, but like so many other BSA designs, perfection was near when the model was dropped from production. Certainly a hard and fast decision had been made to eliminate the Bantam for all time, as Bob Currie has been able to confirm that the jigs were destroyed by sledge hammer to prevent a later resurrection. A pity, because by that time it is reasonable to assume that something like 500,000 Bantams had been made in the UK alone, which must surely have represented a most successful venture, even in terms of BSA production levels.

H.6942

EVOLUTION

It took less than four months after BSA had announced, early in 1948, that they would make a two-stroke engine only, and not the cycle parts, for the original decision to be changed. It was the only sensible course of action that could have been taken, for the British motorcycle industry needed a new generation of cheap, lightweight machines to meet the demand for civilian models when production resumed after the war. Initially, the export market had prior claim, the war having drained Britain's resources and left the need to repay massive debts. But towards the end of 1948 the D1 model, or Bantam as it had by then been officially named, became generally available. Unlike its American counterpart, which was derived from the same DKW design, the Bantam used a frame and cycle parts that were of BSA design and manufacture. Thus commenced what proved to be one of BSA's most successful postwar ventures.

The one basic model soon became available with a choice of options at extra cost, rectified battery lighting with coil ignition, and a spring frame of the plunger suspension type. It also became possible to obtain a competition version, basically a standard D1 model that had been modified in certain respects to make it more suitable for use in trials-type events. Production continued with only minor changes, which in 1953 included the option of an all-black finish instead of the familiar Mist Green. A year later the cylinder head and barrel were given more generous fins, whilst the standard model lost one of its basic recognition features, the flat fishtail silencer, which continued on the competition model only. In its place a cylindrical silencer with detachable baffles and a fishtail end formed the replacement. 1954 marked the introduction of the 148cc Bantam Major, which had been on display at the 1953 Earls Court Show. The capacity increase had been brought about by the simple expedient of increasing the cylinder bore size, to give bore and stroke dimensions of 57 x 58mm. Given a D3 coding, the new model complemented the smaller capacity Bantams and could also be obtained in competition form, but with a plunger-sprung frame only. The most distinguishing feature of the D3 models was the Pastel Grey finish.

The colour option of the D1 models was extended still further during 1955 by offering a maroon finish, but only a year later production of the rigid frame version finally came to an end. Orders from the Post Office and other governmental channels for the plunger suspension model kept this version of the D1 going until 1963. 1956 also marked the end of production of the 123cc and 148cc competition models, and of the plunger sprung D3, which was now superseded by a swinging arm version. A dualseat fitted to the new model replaced the old and more conventional saddle, not quite so necessary with more effective rear suspension.

Production of the D3 model came to an end in late 1957, the 173cc Bantam Super having made its debut at the end of 1957. Listed under the D5 coding, the increase in capacity had again been achieved by opening out the cylinder bore still further: bore and stroke dimensions now being 61.5 x 58mm. Finished in maroon, or with the option of black, the Bantam Super had a power output of almost $7\frac{1}{2}$bhp as compared to the 4bhp rating of the original D1 model. A particularly interesting feature was a change that had been made in the lubrication system, whereby oil from the gearbox was used to lubricate the left-hand main bearing of the crankshaft assembly, a bleed from the primary chaincase performing a similar function in the case of the right-hand bearing. A tendency for the main bearings to rust as a result of condensation had prompted the need for more positive lubrication in this area and to rationalise production, the crankcase assembly of the D1 model followed suit.

Unlike its predecessors, the D5 model had only a relatively short production life, for on the eve of the 1958 Show the 173cc D7 model took its place. Distinguishing features included a modified frame with rear suspension similar to that of BSA's 250cc four-stroke, strengthened telescopic forks with hydraulic damping, and a two-tone finish in Black and Royal Red. Unnoticed was the way in which the overall weight of the Bantam was slowly edging up, the D7 weighing-in at 224lb compared with the 160lb of the original rigid frame D1. An increase in brake drum diameter to $5\frac{1}{2}$ inches, front and rear, helped the brakes keep pace with the increase in power output and weight.

1962 saw the introduction of a needle roller bearing assembly for the small end, the D1 model being phased out of production a year later. Production of the D7 model continued, with minor modifications, until 1965, when the big-end bearing was modified and the internal gear ratios changed. A De-Luxe version with improved lighting and cosmetic attention to the petrol tank and seat in particular became available at the same time. This, however, was only a prelude to the discontinuation of the standard D7 later in the year, it being replaced by what was known as the Silver model, of similar specification to the De-Luxe but embodying certain economies that reduced the retail price. By the middle of 1966, both versions of the D7 had been superseded by the D10 Bantam Supreme and the D10 Silver.

Of all the years during which the Bantam was in production, 1966 can truly be regarded as 'the year of the Bantam', for in addition to the two models already mentioned, two others were listed. These comprised the D10 Sports, a 4-speed D10 that took on the appearance of a mini-racer, with a humped seat, dropped bars, flyscreen, high level exhaust and even chequered tape, and the D10 Bushman. The Bushman was particularly interesting, being what amounted to a trail bike version of the Bantam. It proved to be a particularly attractive-looking bike, with its orange-coloured tank, upswept exhaust system and crankcase undershield. It too had a four-speed gearbox, and lowered gear ratios. By now, it was apparent that the model coding bore a direct relationship to the power output of the engine, for the D10 models produced 10bhp at 6000rpm. This amounted to a 40% increase over that produced by the earlier D7 model, and was brought about by re-porting the engine, increasing the compression ratio and by once again fitting discs to the flywheels to increase crankcase compression. The sports model would reach in excess of 60mph,

without any noticeable loss of bottom end torque or lack of smoothness. All models had the contact breaker assembly on the right-hand side, access to which was gained via a circular cover plate in the primary chaincase cover, a larger alternator, a four plate clutch to handle the extra power, and an oval section connecting rod. Japanese influence was shown by the fitting of mirrors to the handlebars.

The D10 models faded out during 1967, to be replaced by the D14/4 series – three models in this instance, all with 4-speed gearboxes. Apart from a further boost in power output (at the expense of some flexibility this time) the specification was similar to that of the 4-speed D10 apart from the use of a larger diameter exhaust pipe. The D14/4S Sports model had the refinement of more sturdy front forks, an attribute shared by the D14/4B Bushman. Sadly, these were the last Bantam models to be sold in significant numbers, for the invasion by lightweight machines from the Orient was beginning to gain a stranglehold on the once seemingly impregnable British market.

The D175 model represented the end of the line, being equipped with a new cylinder head recognisable by its central sparking plug. It also had new crankcases

and heavier front forks, as well as rear suspension units with exposed springs. The headlamp was mounted as a separate unit and assembly had gone over to the use of Unified threads. Two versions of the D175 model were available, the standard road machine and the Bushman.

Sales of lightweight British motorcycles had now reached a very low level, and despite the introduction of the two D175 models in 1969, the Bushman was discontinued towards the end of the following year. The standard model lingered on for only a short while longer, before it too was discontinued during March 1971. By early 1972, the mighty BSA empire had collapsed completely, making the Bantam and all the other models in the BSA range little more than memories. Even so, a production run of something like 500,000 Bantams, from beginning to end, had made its mark. Whoever decided that BSA should look again at the two-stroke, despite the disastrous consequences of the 1927 project, had most certainly made the right decision on this occasion.

SPECIFICATION

D1, D1 Competition and D3 Major

Model number	D1	D1 Competition	D3 Major
Bore and stroke (mm)	52 x 58	52 x 58	57 x 58
Cubic capacity (cc)	123	123	148
Compression ratio	6.5:1	6.5:1	6.4:1
BHP	4 @ 5000rpm	4 @ 5000rpm	5.3 @ 5000rpm
Gear ratios			
4th	–	–	–
3rd	7.0:1	8.65:1	7.0:1
2nd	11.7:1	14.50:1	11.7:1
1st	22.1:1	27.10:1	22.0:1
Sprocket sizes			
Engine	17	17	17
Clutch	38	38	38
Final drive	15	15	15
Rear wheel	47	58	47
Suspension			
Front	Teles	Teles	Teles
Rear	Rigid[1]	Rigid[1]	Plunger[6]
Tyre sizes			
Front	2.75 x 19	2.75 x 19	2.75 x 19
Rear	2.75 x 19	3.25 x 19	2.75 x 19
Brake drum diameter			
Front	5in	5in	$5\frac{1}{2}$in
Rear	5in	5in	5in
Chain size			
Front	$\frac{3}{8} \times \frac{1}{4}$in	$\frac{3}{8} \times \frac{1}{4}$in	$\frac{3}{8} \times \frac{1}{4}$in
Rear	$\frac{1}{2} \times \frac{5}{16}$in	$\frac{1}{2} \times \frac{5}{16}$in	$\frac{1}{2} \times \frac{5}{16}$in
Fuel tank capacity	1.65 gall (Imp)	1.75 gall (Imp)	1.75 gall (Imp)
Petroil mixing ratio	1:24[2]	1:24[2]	1:24[2]
Gearbox oil capacity (cc)	425	425	425
Generator type	ac alternator[3]	ac alternator	ac alternator
Output (watts)	30[4]	30	30
Battery capacity (amp/hr)	5[5]	–	–
Points gap (in)	0.015	0.015	0.015

Ignition timing (BTDC)	$\frac{5}{32}$in	$\frac{5}{32}$in	$\frac{5}{32}$in
Wheelbase (in)	50	50	50
Ground clearance (in)	4.75 t	7.0	4.75
Seat height (in)	27	29	27
Overall width (in)	26.5	26.5	26.5
Dry weight (lb)	153	166	183
Years of manufacture	1948-63	1948-56	1954-7[6]

D3 Competition, D5 Super, D7 Standard and D7 De Luxe

Model number	D3 Competition	D5 Super	D7 Std. & De Luxe
Bore and stroke (mm)	57 x 58	61.5 x 58	61.5 x 58
Cubic capacity (cc)	148	173	173
Compression ratio	6.4:1	7.4:1	7.4:1
Bhp	5.3 @ 5000rpm	7.4 @ 4750rpm	7.4 @ 4750rpm
Gear ratios			
4th	–	–	–
3rd	8.64:1	6.43:1	6.6:1
2nd	14.45:1	10.76:1	9.3:1
1st	27.1:1	20.2:1	17.4:1
Sprocket sizes			
Engine	17	17	17
Clutch	38	38	38
Final drive	15	16	16
Rear wheel	58	46	46
Suspension			
Front	Teles	Teles	Teles
Rear	Rigid	S/arm	S/arm
Tyre sizes			
Front	2.75 x 19	3.00 x 18	3.00 x 18
Rear	3.25 x 19	3.00 x 18	3.00 x 18
Brake drum diameter			
Front	5in	5in	$5\frac{1}{2}$in
Rear	5in	5in	$5\frac{1}{2}$in
Chain size			
Front	$\frac{3}{8}$ x $\frac{1}{4}$in	$\frac{3}{8}$ x $\frac{1}{4}$in	$\frac{3}{8}$ x $\frac{1}{4}$in
Rear	$\frac{1}{2}$ x$\frac{5}{16}$in	$\frac{1}{2}$ x $\frac{5}{16}$in	$\frac{1}{2}$ x $\frac{5}{16}$in
Fuel tank capacity	1.75 gall (Imp)	2.0 gall (Imp)	2.0 gall (Imp)
Petroil mixing ratio	1:24[2]	1:24[2]	1:24[2]
Gearbox oil capacity (cc)	425	425	425
Generator type	ac alternator	ac alternator	ac alternator
Output (watts)	30	30	30
Battery capacity (amp/hr)	–	11	11
Points gap (in)	0.015	0.015	0.015
Ignition timing (BTDC)	$\frac{5}{32}$in	$\frac{5}{32}$in	$\frac{1}{16}$
Wheelbase (in)	50	52	51.1
Ground clearance (in)	7.0	5.5	5.5
Seat height (in)	29	31	31
Overall width (in)	26.5	26.5	27.75
Dry weight (lb)	176	216	224
Years of manufacture	1954-6	1958	1959-66

D10 Supreme, D10 Silver, D10 Sports and D10 Bushman

Model number	D10 Supreme & Silver	D10 Sports	D10 Bushman
Bore and stroke (mm)	61.5 x 58	61.5 x 58	61.5 x 58
Cubic capacity (cc)	173	174	173
Compression ratio	8.65:1	8.65:1	8.65:1
Bhp	10 @ 6000rpm	10 @ 6000rpm	10 @ 6000rpm
Gear ratios			
4th	–	6.58:1	8.1:1
3rd	6.6:1	8.55:1	10.5:1
2nd	9.3:1	12.04:1	14.8:1
1st	17.4:1	18.68:1	23.0:1
Sprocket sizes			
Engine	17	17	17
Clutch	38	38	38
Final drive	16	16	16
Rear wheel	47	47	58
Suspension			
Front	Teles	Teles	Teles
Rear	S/arm	S/arm	S/arm
Tyre sizes			
Front	3.00 x 18	3.00 x 18	3.00 x 19
Rear	3.00 x 18	3.00 x 18	3.00 x 19
Brake drum diameter			
Front	$5\frac{1}{2}$in	$5\frac{1}{2}$in	$5\frac{1}{2}$in
Rear	$5\frac{1}{2}$in	$5\frac{1}{2}$in	$5\frac{1}{2}$in
Chain size			
Front	$\frac{3}{8} \times \frac{1}{4}$in	$\frac{3}{8} \times \frac{1}{4}$in	$\frac{3}{8} \times \frac{1}{4}$in
Rear	$\frac{1}{2} \times \frac{5}{16}$	$\frac{1}{2} \times \frac{5}{16}$	$\frac{1}{2} \times \frac{5}{16}$
Fuel tank capacity	1.9 gall (Imp)	1.9 gall (Imp)	1.9 gall (Imp)
Petroil mixing ration	$1:24^2$	$1:24^2$	$1:24^2$
Gearbox oil capacity (cc)	425	425	425
Generator type	ac alternator	ac alternator	ac alternator
Output (watts)	60	60	60
Battery capacity (amp/hr)	11	11	11
Points gap (in)	0.012	0.012	0.012
Ignition timing (BTDC)	$\frac{1}{16}$in	$\frac{1}{16}$in	$\frac{1}{16}$in
Wheelbase (in)	50	50	50
Ground clearance (in)	6.75	6.75	10.5
Seat height (in)	31	30.25	30.5
Overall width (in)	27.75	23	27.75
Dry weight (lb)	215	221	222
Years of manufacture	1966-7	1966-7	1966-7

D14/4. D14/4 Sports, D175 and D14/4 Bushman

Model number	D14/4, D14/4 Sports and D175	D14/4 Bushman
Bore and stroke (mm)	61.5 x 58	61.5 x 58
Cubic capacity (cc)	173	173
Compression ratio	10:1	10:1
Bhp	12.6 @ 5.750rpm	12.6 @ 5.750rpm

Gear ratios

4th	6.58:1	8.1:1
3rd	8.55:1	10.5:1
2nd	12.04:1	14.8:1
1st	18.68:1	23.0:1

Sprocket sizes

Engine	17	17
Clutch	38	38
Final drive	16	16
Rear wheel	47	58

Suspension

Front	Teles	Teles
Rear	S/arm	S/arm

Tyre sizes

Front	3.00 x 18	3.00 x 19
Rear	3.00 x 18	3.25 x 18

Brake drum diameter

Front	$5\frac{1}{2}$in	$5\frac{1}{2}$in
Rear	$5\frac{1}{2}$in	$5\frac{1}{2}$in

Chain size

Front	$\frac{3}{8}$ x $\frac{1}{4}$in	$\frac{3}{8}$ x $\frac{1}{4}$in
Rear	$\frac{1}{2}$ x $\frac{5}{16}$	$\frac{1}{2}$ x $\frac{5}{16}$

Fuel tank capacity	1.9 gall (Imp)	1.9 gall (Imp)
Petroil mixing ratio	1:24 [2]	1:24 [2]
Gearbox oil capacity (cc)	425	425
Generator type	ac alternator	ac alternator
Output (watts)	60	60
Battery capacity (amp/hr)	11	11
Points gap (in)	0.012	0.012
Ignition timing (BTDC)	$\frac{1}{16}$in	$\frac{1}{16}$in
Wheelbase (in)	50	50
Ground clearance (in)	6.75	10
Seat height (in)	31	30.5
Overall width (in)	27.75	27.75
Dry weight (lb)	215	222
Years of manufacture	1968-71	1968-71

Notes

1 *Plunger frame available as an option*
2 *Ratio using self-mixing oil*
3 *Option of generator with rectifier and battery lighting*
4 *Output from Wico-Pacy 'Geni-Mag' alternator*
5 *Battery fitted to rectifier lighting systems only*
6 *Plunger suspension superseded by swinging arm type in 1956*

Carburettors

Model	Type and specification	Choke size	Main jet	Pilot jet	Slide No.	Needle position
D1 models 1948-50	Amal 261/001D	$\frac{5}{8}$in	75	–	5	2
D1 models 1951-63	Amal 361/1	$\frac{5}{8}$in	75	–	5	2
D3 models 1954-58	Amal 523/7	$\frac{11}{16}$in	90	–	5	3

D5 and D7 models (1958-66)	Amal Monobloc 375/31	$\frac{7}{8}$in	140	25	$3\frac{1}{2}$	2
D10 and D14/4 models also D175 (1967-71)	Amal Concentric R626/2	26mm	150	25	3	2
Bushman D10 and D14/4 models (1967-71)	Amal Concentric R626/17	26mm	160	25	3	2

Note: Main jet sizes vary from 150 on D10 models to 180 on D175. D14/4 models have 160 main jet and needle in No. 2 position. All use 0.105 needle jet except D1 (0.106), D3 (0.107) and D7 (0.106). Some variations in needle position may be necessary to suit individual engine characteristics. Count position from TOP.

H.6942

ROAD TESTS

MOTOR CYCLING ROAD TESTS

The 123 c.c. Model D1
B.S.A. "BANTAM"

A Spring-frame-equipped Edition of a Famous Two-stroke Fitted With Rectified A.C. Lighting

Although an ultra-lightweight, the B.S.A. "Bantam" accommodates a six-foot rider in comfort. Note the extensive mudguard valancing fore and aft.

(Right) This offside view of the machine emphasizes its attractive lines. On the streamlined crankcase-gearbox housing will be seen the gearchange and kickstarter pedals operating on a common axis.

FEW machines have been greeted by the large body of lightweight users with as much enthusiasm as was accorded to the introduction of the "Bantam." This 123 c.c. mount, with its modernistic lines, essentially practical specification, and "fetching" pale green and fawn colour scheme, seemed to "fill the bill" in every particular. In 1950, however, the makers decided to accede to the requests of one particular class of "Bantam" users. These were the folk who found the performance of their machines to be so good that they put their mounts to tasks that would normally have been done by a much higher-powered motorcycle—long-distance touring, sustained good-average rides over give and take roads, and much night driving.

For this kind of hard work the standard D1 model was deemed capable of some modification and, following the post-war trend, its manufacturers offered, as optional specification additions, a rear springing system, designed to ease the way of hard-riding owners, and a battery lighting set for those whose travelling included much after-dark roadfaring. Thus, the machine can now be fitted with

either of these features, or with both, and it was a mount having the new lighting set and the rear springing system that *Motor Cycling* road-tested.

Apart from the Lucas A.C. generator, the engine is similar to the one road-tested in a rigid frame in 1948. A cast-iron barrel is bolted to the egg-shaped shell containing the crank assembly, primary transmission and three-speed gearbox. The bore and stroke are 52 mm. and 58 mm. respectively, giving a swept volume of 123 c.c. The deflectorless piston has a diametrically gashed skirt, whilst the two transfer ports are disposed at 180 degrees. Four full-length studs retain the aluminium alloy cylinder head and the 14-mm. sparking plug is screwed in at an angle of approximately 45 degrees, with the points facing the exhaust port. The foot-change gear-lever and kickstarter spindles are concentric, the gear position indicator operating on the near side of the machine.

The loop frame enclosing the engine-gearbox unit has most of its joints welded and the light, telescopic forks of B.S.A. design, are now fitted with telescoping rubber dust covers and carry a W.M.1-19-in. wheel with a 2.75 by 19-in. Dunlop tyre. Taking the place of the welded rear spindle lugs, two forgings, also welded to the rear frame loop, carry the rear suspension slider rods. Movement of the spindle lugs on their rods is controlled, in deflection and rebound, by coil springs neatly encased in telescopic covers.

In place of the flywheel magneto, with its direct lighting coil, is the Lucas A.C. generator, built into the near-side of the crankcase and supplying current to a Lucas battery through a metal rectifier housed alongside the toolbox. Ignition is now by coil, with the contact breaker embodied in the generator unit and the coil placed in a well-protected position on the top frame tube under the petroil tank. Controlling the ignition and lighting circuits, a moulded plastic switch is fitted in the head lamp shell, the ignition switch being operated by a detachable key, as in car practice.

As is customary with road-testers, the first action on taking over the machine was to examine to what extent it could be made to fit the rider's stature. It was found that the handlebars are clamped to the head fork and are adjustable for height, but as the clutch and front-brake controls are pivoted on lugs welded to the bars themselves, there is a limit to the range of movement which can be obtained here. In spite of this, however, it was found that the levers are comfortably placed and within natural reach. The foot-rests are not adjustable and, with a fairly low saddle position, give the impression that the lay-out has been designed expressly for users of average height—those who are long legged may find this a point for some criticism, though splines enable the angle of the foot-change lever to be adjusted, and personal whim in this department can be satisfied.

The recent extremely cold weather brought no starting difficulties, the effortless "commencement" bringing home to the tester the fact that here alone is a point that must make a strong appeal to riders who find that 350 c.c. or 500 c.c. machines are above their capabilities. A combined air-cleaner and choke is fitted to the

Amal type 261/001D carburetter, and the choke could, in a very short time, be opened fully as the engine warmed up. When hot, one gentle prod was all that was necessary to bring the machine to life.

Bottom gear could be selected without noise, for the clutch freed entirely and showed no sign of drag, while the easy and light movement of the control ensured smooth engagement. Gear changes could be made with certainty and without noise, only the gentlest pressure being necessary to move the pedal over its range of movement. Top gear could be used down to 17 or 18 m.p.h., and at this speed, even when pulling only lightly, the engine continued to two-stroke without hesitation. It was, of course, preferable to engage second gear when accelerating away from this speed, but on level roads the flexibility of the engine was such that no protest was forthcoming if top gear was held. Under normal conditions, the best speeds at which to make changes of gear were found to be 10 m.p.h. from bottom, and 25 m.p.h. from second. A cruising speed of 40 m.p.h. could be maintained without the slightest sign of complaint, the engine appearing to be perfectly happy at this gait, i.e., 3,770 r.p.m. which represents an approximate piston speed of 1,450 ft. per min.

Very varied weather conditions provided opportunities to sample the excellent roadholding and stability of the machine on vastly different road surfaces. On ice and snow, for example, the weight of a motorcycle is a factor which looms large in the mind of its rider, and the fact that the "Bantam" scales only 168 lb. was a considerable comfort to the tester in these circumstances. Although riding "prepared to foot," the necessity did not arise and some measure of the great confidence felt must have been derived from this. Again, in the negotiation of traffic, low weight, together with a good steering lock, are of primary importance and the "Bantam" could be threaded through busy streets with complete confidence in the satisfying knowledge that ill-conditioned tram lines and greasy city surfaces would provoke no awkward situations.

(Right) The simple but effective method by which the rear of the machine is sprung.

(Below) A particularly easily operated central stand forms part of the "Bantam's" equipment.

(Below) Accessible adjustment of the make - and - break points on the built-in Lucas A.C. generator is a feature.

MOTOR CYCLING ROAD TESTS

BRIEF SPECIFICATION OF THE 123 c.c. MODEL D1 "BANTAM" B.S.A.

Engine: Single-cylinder B.S.A. two-stroke; 52 mm. bore by 58 mm. stroke; deflectorless aluminium-alloy piston; twin transfer ports; roller bearing big-end, detachable alloy cylinder head; crankshaft runs in ball-journal bearings with spring-loaded seals; petroil lubrication; Amal carburetter with combined air cleaner and choke; twist-grip control; ignition by coil with Lucas flywheel generator.

Gearbox: Constant mesh, built in unit with engine; ratios 7.0, 11.7 and 22.0 to 1; operation by built-in positive stop foot control with gear-position indicator; primary drive by .375-in. pitch chain, rear chain ½ in. by .335 in.; three-plate clutch; kickstarter working on common spindle with gear-control pedal.

Frame: Welded loop construction with B.S.A. telescopic front forks and plunger-type rear suspension; spring-up central stand; adjustable handlebars; sprung front mudguard; deep valances to both mudguards; rear carrier; square toolbox with detachable lid, fastened with two coin-slotted, knurled, dome-nuts; 1⅞-gallon petrol tank; oil measure contained in filler cap.

Wheels: Fitted with Dunlop 2.75-in. by 19-in. tyres; 5-in. diameter brakes with finger adjustment to controls; non-adjustable bearings.

Equipment: Lucas 6v. A.C. generator supplying current through a rectifier to a Lucas battery, ignition and light switches mounted on head lamp; Lucas h.f. electric horn; Smiths 55 m.p.h. speedometer.

Finish: Frame, forks, tank, wheels, etc., in pastel green, cream tank panels, bright parts chrome plated.

Dimensions: Wheelbase, 50 ins.; saddle height, 27 ins.; ground clearance, 4¾ ins.; overall width, 26½ ins.; overall length, 77 ins.; weight, 168 lb.

Annual Tax: 17s. 6d. (4s. 10d. quarterly).

Price: In standard form, £63 3s. 6d., plus £17 1s. 2d. purchase tax; spring frame, £5 (plus £1 7s. purchase tax) extra; Lucas generator and battery lighting, £6 plus £1 12s. 5d. purchase tax extra.

Makers: B.S.A. Cycles, Ltd., Small Heath, Birmingham.

Both the front and rear suspension systems worked in an exemplary fashion. The total movement on the front forks is just under 5 ins. and this degree of deflection copes adequately with all road conditions. Approximately half this amount of movement is available at the rear to provide a comfortable ride, entirely free from the pitching that is, at times, apparently inseparable from short-wheelbase, lightweight mounts. In fact, it is true to say that much of the general all-round stability of the rear-sprung "Bantam" is due to the way in which the rear wheel sticks to the road.

The front and rear brakes were found to be both fully capable of dealing with all eventualities likely to arise and it will be seen from the accompanying test panel that very creditable stopping figures were obtained. Straight-line braking was the rule; even with the severest pressure, the rear wheel locked only when the shoes were fiercely applied. It was thought that a greater degree of sensitivity might have been possible if the rear brake could have been applied without removing the foot from the rest, though this is perhaps a rather pedantic criticism in view of the general excellence of the braking performance. Adjustment of the front anchor was made simple by a knurled thumb-wheel and could be effected in a matter of seconds; a wing nut copes with the rear brake in a similar fashion.

The improved lighting system was found to make night riding almost as comfortable as daytime cruising and, with the full beam in use, no difficulty was experienced in maintaining the normal road speed. The handlebar switch mounted close to the clutch lever, in an easily operated position, controls the dipping arrangement and when in the "dipped" position produces an unusually flat bar of light which ensures that oncoming traffic is not inconvenienced by dazzle. Advantage is taken of the provision of a battery by mounting a Lucas electric horn instead of the bulb horn located in the steering head on the standard "Bantam."

Excellent petroil consumption figures were to be expected and those obtained are indeed outstanding. The test run was made over average going. The road speed was maintained at the figure indicated in the test panel up hill and down.

The graph indicates that, while 35 m.p.h. is attained fairly quickly, the climb to maximum speed is affected considerably by increased wind resistance. In second gear at maximum speed, the comparatively short stroke ensures that piston speed is kept down and at 5,860 r.p.m. it is only 2,240 ft. per min. Even at maximum revs. in top it is well below 2,000 ft. per min. This should ensure good wearing qualities and a considerable mileage before piston and barrel need attention. All figures shown have been corrected for speedometer error, which proved to be progressively fast through the range.

Some misuse of the clutch is unavoidable when obtaining graph figures, but the "Bantam" unit stood up very well.

The deep valances on the mudguards did their job efficiently, little road dirt finding its way on to rider or machine. Oil leaks are non-existent, the only evidence of extraneous lubricant being a few spots on the bottom chain-guard.

Routine attentions are extremely easy to carry out. Contact points are revealed when the two screws holding the cover to the generator housing are removed. Clutch adjustment is even simpler and is immediately adjacent to the generator cover plate. Grease nipples are liberally provided at all points needing this attention. Battery topping-up can be done so soon as the retaining strap is removed. The coil is, of course, in the interests of waterproofing and safety, not easily got at, but the high-tension-lead terminal can be detached without removing the petroil tank.

The equipment is comprehensive, a sturdy carrier, capable of withstanding any weight likely to be carried, is fitted to the rear mudguard. Tucked away under the petroil tank is the tyre pump, well clear of road dirt. A tubular central stand, easily operated, is hinged on the footrest mounting.

In conclusion it can be said without fear of contradiction that the latest D1 refinements so enhance the performance and usefulness of an already highly popular machine that it is fully assured of an even wider following of enthusiastic admirers. Its creators, the B.S.A. Cycle Co., Ltd., Small Heath, Birmingham, may well feel proud of the manner in which the "Bantam" has won its spurs.

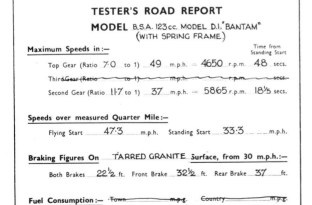

TESTER'S ROAD REPORT

MODEL B.S.A. 123 c.c. MODEL D.1. "BANTAM" (WITH SPRING FRAME.)

Maximum Speeds in:—

Top Gear (Ratio 7.0 to 1) ....49... m.p.h. = 4650 r.p.m. 48 secs.

~~Third Gear (Ratio ... to 1) ... m.p.h. = ... r.p.m. ... secs.~~

Second Gear (Ratio 11.7 to 1) 37 m.p.h. = 5865 r.p.m. 18⅕ secs.

Speeds over measured Quarter Mile:—

Flying Start 47.3 m.p.h. Standing Start 33.3 m.p.h.

Braking Figures On TARRED GRANITE Surface, from 30 m.p.h.:—

Both Brakes 22½ ft. Front Brake 32½ ft. Rear Brake 37 ft.

Fuel Consumption:— ~~Town m.p.g.~~ ~~Country m.p.g.~~

30 M.P.H. —179 M.P.G. 40 M.P.H. — 115 M.P.G.

Oil Consumption:— NOT APPLICABLE m.p.g.

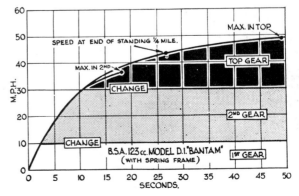

THE B.S.A. " Bantam " Model D1 was first produced in August, 1948, as an " export only " model, but after a short period, during which it became extremely popular in the overseas market, it was released for home sales. It made its bow in this country at the 1948 Show. Since then it has been produced in enormous quantities. The type is in use in 78 different overseas markets. At home this little machine, with its striking colour scheme of mist green with cream tank panels, has become one of the most familiar motorcycles on our roads. The " Bantam " appeared originally with an all-welded tubular loop frame, with the engine/gear unit housed in simple cradle lugs, and the specification included Wico-Pacy direct lighting with flywheel magneto together with telescopic front forks. The model in this form is still listed, but extra items of specification at an additional charge now include plunger-type rear suspension and Lucas A.C. generator lighting set. These made their appearance for the 1950 season, while at the same time the Competition model was announced in response to public demand. Its immediate success as a trials machine, with upswept exhaust system, special gear ratios, folding kick-starter and other items considered desirable for this class of work, is of particular interest. Furthermore, it is now lending itself to much " private-owner " experimental work for racing, and both " Bantams " entered in the 1951 Ultra-Lightweight T.T. completed the course.

G. Beresford

Technical Details

Engine : Single-cylinder two-stroke ; bore, 52 mm. ; stroke, 58 mm., equalling 123 c.c. ; light-alloy detachable cylinder head and cast-iron barrel ; slightly domed aluminium alloy deflectorless piston with two compression rings ; single induction and exhaust ports ; twin tangential transfer ports for high efficiency filling and scavenging ; alloy steel connecting rod with bushed small-end for floating gudgeon pin ; single-row roller big-end, uncaged ; light internal flywheels of forged steel, incorporating bob-weights and faced with steel discs to provide smooth exterior and ensure adequate crankcase compression ; crankpin and mainshafts press-fit in flywheels ; drive side mainshaft mounted on two ball journal

bearings, with spring-loaded oil and pressure seal interposed ; other mainshaft mounted on a single ball-bearing, and carrying flywheel magneto (or A.C. generator) in a separate compartment with oil seal between ; petroil lubrication ; Amal single lever carburetter with strangler for cold starting.

Transmission : Gearbox built in unit construction with engine, primary drive in separate compartment, with oil-tight die-cast aluminium cover, from taper and key-mounted sprocket on engine mainshaft by ⅜-in. pitch roller chain to clutch coupled by splines to gearbox mainshaft ; clutch has three driven plates with cork inserts and four steel driving plates, the outermost of which also serves as the pressure plate and takes the thrust provided by six helical compression springs ; clutch operation by steel thrust-rod, through hollow gearbox mainshaft, pressing against the thrust-plate centre

Wheels: Fitted Dunlop tyres, 2.75 by 19 ins.; hubs fitted with non-adjustable ball journal bearings; 5-in. brakes, both with finger adjustment.

Electical Equipment: Wico-Pacy direct lighting set, comprising flywheel magneto with additional coils for head and tail lamps, without accumulator; dry battery mounted in head lamp provides current for pilot and rear lamp when parking: cable-operated switch lever mounted on left handlebar, giving " off," " park," " full " and " dip,"; alternative at an extra charge, Lucas A.C. generator set, with rectifier, accumulator on seat tube, coil ignition, and H.F. electric horn.

General Equipment: Spring-seat saddle; metal toolbox with complete kit, mounted on seat tube; bulb horn on models with Wico-Pacy equipment (H.F. horn with special dry battery, extra); illuminated Smiths speedometer mounted on front fork top bridge, driven from rear wheel.

hrough a large-area mushroom-head contact rod, and actuated at s other end from the control cable by a lever coupled to a quick-hread sleeve, with adjustable pressure pin and hardened steel ontact ball; three-speed constant-mesh gear with positive-stop foot ear-change, having a visible gear-position indicator; gearbox main-haft mounted on ball journal bearings, with a spring-loaded oil al at the output end; kick-starter and foot gear-change lever nounted on a common axis, with ample bearing areas for both; ear drive by ½-in. pitch roller chain from sprocket on nearside of earbox mainshaft to rear wheel sprocket, and protected by top-run hain guard; gear ratios, 7.0, 11.7, 22.0 to 1.

Frame: Self-contained loop type, of all-welded tubular steel con-truction; telescopic front forks with dust-excluding concertina-type ubber gaiters on sliding legs, total travel 3¾ ins.; rear springing, vhen fitted, of plunger type, total movement 2¼ ins.; deeply alanced mudguards; welded steel petrol tank, capacity 1¾ gals.; pring-up central stand; rubber-covered footrests, rear luggage arrier.

Finish: High quality mist-green enamel; tank in mist-green with cream panels; exhaust system and other bright parts, chromium plated.

Dimensions: Wheelbase, 50 ins.; overall length, 77 ins.; overall width, 26½ ins.; saddle height, 27 ins.; ground clearance, 4¼ ins.; dry weight, 153 lb. (with rear suspension, 168 lb.; with Lucas generator set, 10 lb. extra).

Performance: Vide *Motor Cycling* road test, February 9, 1950. Maximum speed, 49 m.p.h. (4,650 r.p.m.); time from standing start to maximum, 48 secs.; speed over flying quarter-mile, 47.3 m.p.h.; standing start, 33.3 m.p.h.; fuel consumption at 30 m.p.h., 179 m.p.g.; at 40 m.p.h., 115 m.p.g.; braking figures on dry road from 30 m.p.h., both brakes, 22½ ft. front brake, 32½ ft.; rear brake, 37 ft.

Competition Model: As standard specification except for cable-operated decompressor in cylinder head; folding kick-starter; adjustable footrests; unvalanced mudguards; raised saddle mounting; rear tyre, 3.25 by 19 ins.; taper roller bearings in front wheel; upswept exhaust system; gear ratios, 8.64, 14.45 and 27.14 to 1.

Makers: B.S.A. Cycles, Ltd., Birmingham, 11.

MOTOR CYCLE, 24 APRIL 1968

173cc BSA BANTAM D14/4

Motor Cycle road test

There can't be so very much wrong with a model which has held a solid place in the affections of the public for 20 years or more—and which is still a best-seller. Of course, the Bantam has changed a bit in that length of time; from a solid frame, through plunger rear springing to the current, orthodox pivoted rear fork, and from the initial 123 cc, through 148 cc to a healthy 173 cc.

And that is by no means the whole story. While growing up in size, it has acquired sophistication and a surprisingly big increase in power output. The long-lived three-speed gearbox has been replaced by a very welcome four-speed assembly, and instead of the former flywheel magneto and direct lighting there is a full alternator-rectifier-battery electrical system.

Minor improvements include a battery which can be kept in good order without the necessity for first detaching the dual-seat, chromium-plated fuel-tank side panels, and two handlebar mirrors fitted as standard. Yet with all this the Bantam continues to be one of the best bargains on the British market, at just over £130. Quite an achievement.

Certainly it's a lightweight—it can be lifted about without trouble when, say, a narrow garden path has to be negotiated—but there is nothing tiddler-like about the frame dimensions. The

Removal of the nearside panel reveals the battery and tool roll

SPECIFICATION

ENGINE: Capacity and type: 173 cc (61.5 x 58mm) two-stroke single. Bearings: Three ball mains, roller big-end. Lubrication: Petroil, 32 to 1 ratio. Mains lubricated from gear box and primary chaincase. Compression ratio: 10 to 1. Carburettor: Amal Concentric R626 (26mm choke). Air slide operated by handlebar lever. Mesh-and-felt air filter. Claimed output: 13 bhp at 5,750 rpm.

TRANSMISSION: Primary by ⅜ x 0.250in chain in oilbath case; secondary by ½in x 0.205in chain. Clutch: Multiplate. Overall gear ratios: 18.68, 12.04, 8.55 and 6.58 to 1. Engine rpm at 30 mph in top gear: 2,800.

ELECTRICAL EQUIPMENT: Ignition by 6-volt battery and coil, with emergency-start circuit. Charging: Wipac 60-watt alternator to 6-volt, 10-amp-hour battery through rectifier. Headlamp: Wipac 5in-diameter with 30/24-watt main bulb.

FUEL CAPACITY: 1⅛ gallons.

TYRES: Dunlop Lightweight studded, 3.00 x 18in front and rear.

BRAKES: 5⅛in diameter front and rear, with finger adjusters.

SUSPENSION: Hydraulically damped telescopic front fork. Pivoted rear fork controlled by Girling spring-and-hydraulic units.

DIMENSIONS: Wheelbase, 50in; ground clearance, 6½in; seat height, 31in. All unladen.

WEIGHT: 215 lb dry.

PRICE: £130 16s 6d, including British purchase tax.

ROAD TAX: £5 a year.

MAKERS: BSA Motor Cycles Ltd, Armoury Road, Small Heath, Birmingham, 11.

PERFORMANCE

(Obtained by "Motor Cycle" staff at MIRA Proving Ground, Lindley, Leicestershire.)

MEAN MAXIMUM SPEED: 64 mph (11½-stone rider wearing two-piece trials suit and boots).

HIGHEST ONE-WAY SPEED: 66 mph (light, following three-quarter wind).

BRAKING: From 30 mph to rest on dry tarmac, 29ft 6in.

TURNING CIRCLE: 12ft 6in.

MINIMUM NON-SNATCH SPEED: 20 mph in top gear.

WEIGHT PER CC: 1.23 lb.

Following pages: the BSA Bantam was developed steadily over the years. The D14/4 led finally to the 1971 Bantam 175 pictured here (*National Motorcycle Museum*)

97

noticeable surge of energy as the revs start to climb from the lower end of the range, and this results in some very respectable acceleration figures — up to 50 mph, that is, for though there is plenty yet to come, it does mean squeezing the bottle to get it.

Keep the motor buzzing (and that's where the four-speed gearbox helps) and the Bantam will soar up a hill with complete contempt for the gradient. Of course, ye olde-tyme Bantam would get to the top, too, in its own sweet time either by clinging doggedly to top cog until it was almost possible to count each rev, or by screaming along in second. The advantage of the new job lies not only in that well-chosen third gear, but also in the throaty, middle-of-the-range supply of urge.

A comfortable cruising speed turned out to be an indicated 60 mph (an actual 57 mph, allowing for speedometer error) but there was more to come, given only moderate encouragement. Running before the wind, it was possible to show slightly better than 70 mph on the dial at times.

Some slight roughness was evident at very low speeds in top gear. But this smoothed out from 30 mph, and in the middle reaches the power flow was as sweet as one could wish for.

Not thirsty

It is a recognised fact that the price of pepping-up a two-stroke is increased fuel consumption. Yet the Bantam is not especially thirsty. Keep it at 30 to 40 mph, and a return of 100 mpg is guaranteed — comforting news for those in search of a light, utterly reliable workhorse for city streets. Only if the throttle is held wide open does the fuel graph take a nose-dive.

The combination of light overall weight, nice balance, a nippy engine and precise steering showed up to the full when a particularly twisty length of B-class road was tackled. Cornering was limited only by the rather low (and non-adjustable) footrests. These are conditions a Bantam rider can enjoy. For although such roads have something less than billiard-table surfaces, the jolts and jars are not passed on to the man in the saddle, thanks to efficient fore and aft suspension.

The electrical system is 6-volt, yet this is quite adequate for the nature of the model, and a particularly good word should be given to the solid and handily-placed dipswitch toggle, easily operated by a gloved hand. As mentioned earlier, the battery has been made more accessible on the D14 4. It is secured by a spring toggle clamp, and may be extracted for in-

riding position is comfortable for both lankies and shorties, and though the 31 in seat height sounds a lot, the model's slimness allows the feet to be put down very confidently at halts.

An air lever is fitted to the handlebar, and for the first start of the morning best results were obtained when this was closed for a few seconds. At other times, it was quite sufficient just to tickle the carburettor.

Lower end

In gaining extra power output, the D14 Bantam has changed its characteristics in some degree, and it is no longer quite the low-speed slogger it used to be. There is a

Very much a two-up machine—a comfortable dualseat, pillion foot-rests and power aplenty

spection and topping-up through an opening in the tool-box backplate, on the left. In theory, this is fine; in practice, extraction is hampered by the nearness of several loose cables draped across the opening.

Fasteners

One good point is the use of two half-turn Dzus fasteners to retain the tool-box lid, instead of the captive nuts which have exasperated a whole decade of Bantam owners. Another is the effective silencer with baffles which can be extracted for cleaning.

Finished in serviceable black (or blue) with white lining on mudguards and tank and bright plated tank side-panels, the D14 4 Bantam is a smart little model which does credit to the long-honoured name. In terms of performance, it is far removed from the original D1 Bantam of 1948, but the family resemblance is unmistakable. And who's to say that there won't be a Bantam with us another 20 years from now?

The large-bore exhaust system just clears the frame's front down tube and protects the contact breaker low-tension lead from stone damage

Bottom-, second- and third-gear figures represent maximum-power revs, 8,000

Large enough for a 500 cc machine! The air-filter element is located behind a panel on the offside

BOTTOM SECOND THIRD TOP

ACCELERATION
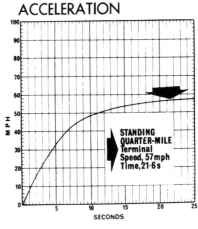
STANDING QUARTER-MILE Terminal Speed, 57mph Time, 21·6 s

FUEL CONSUMPTION
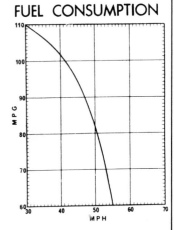

OWNER'S VIEW

Because the BSA Bantam has always been regarded as one of the work horses of the motorcycling world, it is quite difficult to find one that is in 'showroom' original condition, let alone one that has been restored to 'concours' standard. This became only too apparent when the author was seeking out photogenic examples that were to form the basis of the photographic content of this book. It is not difficult to understand why, for the Bantam has yet to have any real collectors' value or even any scarcity rating. Furthermore, there is not the performance aspect nor the charm of a machine that features all manner of unorthodox design characteristics or sets a new trend. Yet for all that, the Bantam has certain indefinable qualities that have endeared it to the hearts of many present and past owners. This makes it all the more interesting to find out why so many examples of this machine have survived, amongst a wide cross-section of motorcycle enthusiasts.

The author's own experiences

The 1955 D3 I obtained was acquired as the result of an impulse buy. I had heard about the machine being available for a quite insignificant sum, although I was warned that it was in dreadful condition, a comment that subsequently proved to be an understatement! But it was basically a plunger frame competition model and it presented a challenge as to whether or not it could be saved.

Virtually every bearing was beyond redemption, including the big-end, which had about $\frac{1}{16}$ inch play! The cylinder barrel was heavily scored and the cylinder head a complete write-off. Incredibly, someone had actually fitted a new 125cc piston into the 150cc cylinder barrel and tried to get the engine to run. The resultant break-up of the piston rings had peppered the combustion chamber and the crown of the piston itself. Other damage was evident in the form of a split fuel tank and the complete exhaust system, footrests, brake pedal and speedometer were missing, as was the saddle. The final indignity was the crude welding on of home-made mudguard stays and what presumably had been intended as shortened footrest stubs. Only the main cycle parts, the basic engine castings and the alternator, gearbox and clutch were suitable for further use.

Surprisingly, parts were not difficult to obtain, and even if I had been rebuilding to as near original specification as possible, this would have presented no difficulty. Overall, the prices for new parts were quite reasonable, whilst in some cases, such as the cylinder barrel, head and handlebars, good second-hand parts helped keep the overall cost of restoration within reasonable bounds. The welded-on bits broke away quite easily and some work with a file removed any remaining traces. Largely, it was a question of stripping and repainting, then reassembling after all the new and replacement parts had been obtained. The opportunity was taken to rebore the newly-acquired cylinder barrel and to fit a new piston (of the correct oversize!) after the flywheel assembly had received its new big end. Nothing really held me up, for it was possible to obtain even a new exhaust system 'over the counter', as well as a replica of the original saddle.

By the time the rebuild had been completed, I estimated that I had spent about six times the purchase price, which at first seemed a little high for a low-priced 'bargain'. But against that I had a fully usable and reliable machine, with an engine that was virtually new within. It might have proved cheaper in the long run to have purchased a machine in better condition, that cost more initially, although I have my doubts. Any second-hand machine invariably needs to have work done on it and unless you are willing to take everything on trust, the only way in which to make sure the machine is sound is to give it a complete overhaul. So I doubt if there is much advantage either way, long term. My bonus was the joy in making something out of nothing and in bending the specification just a trifle to meet my own personal requirements.

I never intended using the machine on the road, as I had no registration documents or even index numbers. I live next to a large wood and, with land of my own, there was no problem in riding the machine off-road as a means of relaxation. As it so happened, this never really came about, although my eldest daughter learnt to ride on it and we would sometimes take it around our field in the summer evenings.

* * *

There is no owners club specifically for Bantam owners, unless the intention is to participate in Bantam racing with a tuned and somewhat modified machine. This is where the Bantam Racing Club comes in. No doubt the BSA Owners Club will cater for Bantam owners, as will the British Two-Stroke Club. I found it was the specialist dealers in BSA spares who could help the most with advice, aided and abetted by the original BSA Service Sheets or manuals that are still relatively easy to obtain. I also gained much useful first-hand experience, which I hope I have been able to pass on, when I wrote the Haynes *BSA Bantam Owners Workshop Manual*.

However, I appreciate that my views are by no means representative of those of the average Bantam owner, so these following comments from others may help give a more balanced view.

John Eyles, the owner of the restored D1 model featured in this book, responded to my questions as follows:

JRC: Why are you so interested in the BSA Bantam?
JWE: Quite simply because the first motorcycle I owned was a hard-saved-for, second-hand BSA Bantam.
JRC: When and why did you buy your Bantam?
JWE: The opportunity came my way in April 1978, when I had no hesitation in buying the machine for total restoration. This was because I have always had an interest in well-restored old machinery.
JRC: What condition was it in and were the faults you found common to the design?
JWE: When purchased, the machine had been partially stripped for use off-road, so the ensuing strip-down was not too difficult. The most serious faults were the complete failure of the electrics, common to most of the early models, and the normal two-stroke chatter of small end and piston slap that became an accepted annoyance to all Bantam onwers.
JRC: What repair/renovation work has been done? Would there have been a better way of tackling the problem as, for example, the purchase of a machine in better or worse condition?

JWE: A total rebuild of the engine and gearbox proved necessary, all the cycle parts being resprayed. Any new part needed was purchased as the restoration continued. In my opinion, the worse condition a machine is in, the better, as one is not tempted to brush over and short cut any of the rebuilding work.
JRC: Have you experienced any difficulty in obtaining parts? If so, what solutions did you find?
JWE: I had difficulty initially, but by following up contacts from a local shop dealing solely in British motorcycles I was able to locate places that still held old BSA parts. Quite a large number were purchased from Bob Joyner, of Birmingham.
JRC: What kind of performance and handling does the machine have?
JWE: The machine looks good and sounds good, but handling can only be described as primitive when compared with modern machines.
JRC: Is your machine in regular use? If so, is this practical and is the running cost high?
JWE: The machine was not renovated to be used, but only to show. The original running cost of these machines was minimal.
JRC: Has your machine won any prizes in Concours or similar events?
JWE: Not yet, as it has not been entered. A bike trailer has yet to be organised to take it to events.
JRC: Do you belong to an owners club or clubs?
JWE: I am not a member of any club yet, although there is a flourishing local club.
JRC: Is there a specialist you have found particularly helpful?
JWE: Bob Joyner, as mentioned earlier. This firm is most helpful with regard to spare parts.
JRC: How would you sum up the enjoyment you get from your Bantam?
JWE: Quite simply, I know of no other Bantam of the same year and of the same type that I have restored. This in itself means a great deal to an owner who realises

he has something that no one else possesses.
JRC: What advice would you give to potential owners of a Bantam?
JWE: Normal restoration costs are high, yet a BSA Bantam can be restored at reasonable cost by the average mechanically-minded enthusiast armed with a good workshop manual. On completion, when the machine is in a position to be viewed by the public, very great interest is shown. This in itself is a great morale booster to any owner.

It is pleasing to find today's younger generation have an interest in restoring old machines, the more so because they see an early Bantam in much the same light as the middle-aged would have seen machines that were manufactured during the twenties. It is easy to forget that when the Vintage MCC was formed in 1946, the youngest machine to qualify for the vintage machine limit would have been only 16 years old! I was fortunate in coming across Timothy Nichol and his father wheeling a pair of restored Bantams into the Classic Bike Show when I arrived there on the opening morning. Only 15 years old, and too young to hold a licence, Timothy's reasons for acquiring and running a Bantam are worth recording:

JRC: Why are you interested in the BSA Bantam?
TN: Because I was brought up with a Bantam, my father having always owned one of these machines. He rode one to work when I was still a baby.
JRC: When and why did you buy your Bantam?
TN: I bought my rigid frame D1 125cc model in May 1981 from a gentleman in Liverpool. I first saw one of these models in a hen house and I thought it would be nice to own an older bike than my Dad. We saw an advertisement in a motorcycle newspaper and my Dad took me to see it, and buy it. He has

owned the D3 model we had at the Show for 20 years and uses it to go to work as well as a general runabout.

JRC: What condition was the machine in, and were the faults you found common to this model?

TN: When purchased, my D1 model had been hand-painted in black and yellow, to cover the rust. All the chrome plating had peeled off, the chainguard had rusted through, the front mudguard had been riveted to hold it together, and the silencer was holed. Only the tyres were in good condition, one of them being an original John Bull 'Deep Grip'. The faults I found are those common to most older bikes – rust and lack of maintenance.

JRC: What repair/renovation work have you carried out? Would there have been a better way of tackling the problem, for example, the purchase of machine in better or worse condition?

TN: I stripped the machine completely, cleaned off all the paint, filled where necessary and then resprayed in the correct colours. The chainguard and mudguards had to be plated and welded, and the seat rebuilt and re-covered. All the plated parts were re-chromed, with the exception of the silencer. This could not be handled because the baffles could not be made clean enough to go into the chrome dip. The engine unit was stripped and the cylinder barrel was rebored and fitted with a new, oversize piston. New oil seals were fitted during the rebuild too. All control cables were renewed and new rubbers were fitted to the handlebars, footrests and gearchange lever.

It would probably have been easier to buy a machine that was in better condition, but this would not have given the same satisfaction.

JRC: Have you experienced any problems in obtaining parts? If so, what solutions did you find?

TN: Most problems were overcome by making parts myself or asking friends to do small specialist jobs for me. I also followed up advertisements in the motorcycling papers and spent many hours of my holidays seeking out old shops and scrap yards.

JRC: What kind of performance and handling does the machine have?

TN: Quite good. With the footrests mounted low to the ground it is sometimes possible to catch one's feet when cornering too steeply. Unfortunately the power output proves too much for the brakes when travelling downhill. The lighting is poor too. But I would not wish to change the bike – except for a Gold Star, which my Dad once owned too!

JRC: Is your machine in regular use? If so, is this practical and are the running costs high?

TN: My age and lack of a licence prevent me from using the machine on the road, although I do ride it in fields. I would expect the running costs to be low with fuel consumption averaging 90mpg.

JRC: Has your machine won prizes in Concours or similar events?

TN: Not yet. The only shows entered have been the 1981 and 1982 Classic Bike Shows.

JRC: Do you belong to an owners club or clubs?

TN: No. There are no clubs for Bantam owners in the North of England or South Scotland, near to where I live.

JRC: Is there a specialist you have found particularly helpful?

TN: Yes, C and D Autos, of Birmingham.

JRC: How would you sum up the enjoyment you get from your Bantam?

TN: It has given great satisaction to restore the bike to its original specification and to be able to ride it. I enjoy hearing tales from older people about the days when they rode a Bantam.

JRC: What advice would you give to a potential owner of a Bantam?

TN: To make sure all the parts are original and that there are no parts missing. Parts are becoming difficult to obtain, and expensive too. Having rebuilt a machine, the owner should take great care of it.

One area in which the Bantam has gained prominence is one that was hardly envisaged when BSA first announced the D1 model – road racing. Yet over the years, Bantam racing has gone from strength to strength, giving a great deal of pleasure to those who enjoy making a standard road machine go fast, and on a limited budget too. Brian Ing is one of many who have raced Bantams in events that cater for the Formula Bantam Racers, and putting his practical experience to good use, he originated The Bantam Tuning Manual, which has become the 'bible' of those who hope to make their Bantam go quickly. His response to my interview maqes interesting reading:

JRC: Why are you interested in the BSA Bantam?

BI: It provides an inexpensive way to go racing and the Bantam Club members are a friendly crowd.

JRC: When and why did you buy your Bantam?

BI: In 1968, to build a Formula Bantam Racer.

JRC: What condition was the machine in, and were the faults found common to this model?

BI: It was a D1 in pieces. The brakes were inadequate for racing and the forks 'flexy' with only 'joke' damping.

JRC: What repair/renovation work have you carried out? Would there have been a better way of tackling the problem, for example, the purchase of a machine in better or worse condition?

BI: The D1 wheels and forks were replaced by D7 parts, which proved adequate for many seasons. The D7 rear wheel is almost universal wear amongst Formula Bantam Racers. The front brake had to be replaced by one that did not fade at Cadwell Park hairpin and most Formula Bantam Racers now use lightweight Japanese discs. The front fork stanchions of a Honda CB125J are the same length and diameter as their D7 counterparts, therefore they fit straight into D7 yokes. The best way to start Formula Bantam racing is to buy a second-hand racer. Currently, they can be purchased quite cheaply, although the cheapest ones would probably need updating to have the advantage of a front disc brake, electronic ignition, large bore carburettor and the latest design exhaust system, etc.

JRC: Have you experienced any problems in obtaining parts? If so, what solution did you find?

BI: Pistons, piston rings and close ratio gear parts have been a problem at different times, but the Bantam Racing Club can boast only one change of Spares Secretary in 14 years. Mick Scutt looked after the Club's needs up to the late 70s, when Martin Baldwin took over. He can still supply all engine and gearbox needs. Cycle parts can be located through the Club magazine or at T&G Motor Cycles, of Thornton Heath, Surrey. Other sources range from bike breakers to autojumbles.

JRC: What kind of performance and handling does the machine have?

BI: 90-100mph, with the fastest Formula Bantam racers reaching around 105mph. My own machine is the only D1 with a rigid rear end that is still being raced regularly, yet it is more than a match for most D3, D5 and D10 models. The only time it seems at a disadvantage is on a bumpy approach to a corner, like the bottom bend at Llandow, mercifully not in current use by the Bantam Racing Club! There are a couple of frames in use that have been modified to mono-shock specification, and they handle very well. The championship winners of recent years have all ridden modified D7 or D10 frames, which have handled very well.

JRC: Has your machine won any prizes?

BI: I have had wins at Debden and Lydden in 1976, at Cadwell Park in 1978 and at Lydden in 1981. Apart from the first win at Debden, the most satisfying results were a third place in the Enduro at Snetterton in 1977, and seventh place in the 1979 and 1980 Bantam Racing Club Championships.

JRC: Do you belong to an owners club or clubs?

BI: I am a member of the Bantam Racing Club. I find the Club magazine particularly helpful, with tuning articles, second-hand spares and the Spares Secretary's list, race results, and regional centre news all making interesting reading. A really well attended Annual General Meeting ensures that the Club is run for the benefit of the racers.

JRC: Is there a specialist you have found particularly helpful?

BI: All the ones I know are particularly helpful, especially Tom Miller, George Harris, Dave Hunter, Mick Scutt, Dave and Trevor Amos, and Jerry Pell.

JRC: How would you sum up the enjoyment you get from your Bantam?

BI: The satisfaction of designing and developing a 125 racer within a formula devised to minimise costs. There is also the satisfaction of quickly becoming competitive in one of the three rider grading classes, and in the racing itself, of course!

JRC: What advice would you give to the potential owner of a Bantam?

BI: First, joint the Bantam Racing Club. Second, buy a second-hand Formula Bantam Racer and Third, get out there and have a go!

Summing up, Brian considers that Bantam racing is a good way in which to gain initial experience on a race track. The novice, intermediate and senior rider gradings ensure at least one race per meeting where the entrant has a good chance of winning. It is also a good way in which to gain experience in preparing competition machines. Understanding the subtleties of a two-stroke competition engine and being able to tune it to get the best from it can only be learned by experience. A single-cylinder engine, such as that of the 125cc Bantam, can provide just that experience, at minimal cost.

H.6942

BUYING

With an estimated half-million Bantams having been manufactured over a span of 23 years, there is no scarcity aspect to inflate the price of machines currently available on the second-hand market. An additional factor that has helped in this respect has been the original low cost of the Bantam and its basic specification, allied with a correspondingly modest performance. Undoubtedly the main pattern of usage was that of providing a cheap and reliable means of travelling to and from work, and there are still quite a number of Bantams fulfilling this role. But one must not forget that the Bantam represented an ideal first bike for the learner rider too, and that many passed from hand to hand in this fashion when the newly-qualified rider purchased a new, and often more powerful, replacement.

Viewed overall, the design was remarkably free of faults as far as average road work was concerned. The very early models had a weak and flimsy centre stand, which would bend very easily and leave the machine balanced precariously with both wheels on the ground. Subsequent modification improved the stand, but it was still prone to suffer from wear around the pivot, with much the same results. Ignition problems

were caused by the alternator rotor hitting the pole pieces of the stator assembly, a fault that was accentuated by worn main bearings. There was also a tendency for the contact breaker points to work loose on their mounting plate, which resulted in an infinitely variable gap and a persistent but difficult to trace misfire or even a complete failure to start and run. As performance increased, the weakness of the front forks began to show up, leading to the need for a more sturdy design with some form of hydraulic damping. It was not until virtually the end of production that the design could be regarded as satisfactory on most counts – and even then, the Bushman models were the ones on which these weaknesses showed up the most. Rear suspension was improved by the use of the swinging arm design: the original plungers barely moved except on heavy impact!

Generally speaking, the lighting system was not too much of a problem on account of the general level of performance of the machine. Even so, the system was uprated as performance increased and although never outstandingly good, the later systems were adequate.

From all of this, it follows that regular routine maintenance was a necessity if the machine was to be kept in serviceable condition, as is the case with any motorcycle. Two-strokes are particularly susceptible to blockage of the exhaust system due to the oily nature of the exhaust gases, and a regular clean out of both the exhaust pipe and silencer was necessary at regular intervals to prevent a gradual drop-off in performance. The silencer had detachable baffles (except the original flat fishtail type) to aid this task.

As far as values are concerned, it is the earlier machines that can be expected to attract the better prices, especially the now somewhat rare Lucas alternator D1 models. The

acquisition of a Bantam does mean that in many cases the rider can enter classic machine events, the Vintage Motor Cycle Club in particular having a 25 year old minimum qualification as the term for entry at the time of publication. It is therefore possible to take part in such events with quite a small capital outlay, unlike the four figures plus required for the older machines and particularly those in the vintage and veteran categories. This factor alone may influence the price of D1 and D3 models as they become more difficult to obtain.

As is so often the case, it is the competition models that are the most sought-after, as they were made in smaller numbers and can still be used in some of the pre-1965 competition events being run in various parts of the country. Sadly, the early beginnings of schoolboy events brought these models into prominence and helped dispose of quite a number by causing them to be ridden into the ground. Another model that can be expected to have a better value is the last in the range, the D175. Due to the penetration of the lightweight Japanese models at that time, comparatively few were sold. Scarcity is always the major factor in forcing up prices.

Yet for all that has been said, any Bantam still represents a very cheap acquisition compared to other contemporary machines. There are very few 30 year old motorcycles that can be purchased for anything like an equivalent sum.

Inevitably the question will arise whether to buy as good a machine as possible, or whether to buy one cheaply, that is known to require attention, in order to undertake a complete rebuild. As mentioned earlier, neither approach has any particular advantage as spare parts are still relatively easy to obtain and at moderate prices too. The only exception occurs if the machine is to be used for Bantam racing events. Under these circumstances it is probably better to acquire a machine that requires attention as only the basic parts are likely to be needed in view of the race modifications that will need to be made if the finished machine is to be competitive. But make sure a copy of the regulations relating to Bantam racing is obtained first, as these will clearly define what can, and what cannot, be modified.

As far as finding a suitable Bantam is concerned, advertisements in the local newspaper or shop windows can usually prove quite fruitful. The alternative is to look through the advertisement section of the more popular motorcycling newspapers and magazines, or specialist advertising weeklies such as *Exchange and Mart.* The classic motorcycle type of magazines cater for this type of machine in their advertising pages too, but in this instance prices are likely to be speculative and in consequence a little higher; the advertiser having realised the potential in having an elderly British motorcycle. This also applies to auctions, where bids made on the spur of the moment can falsely inflate values. The once most prolific source of second-hand Bantams – the Post Office – has by now just about dried up completely, the more so now that the telegram in its original form, and with its implied urgency, no longer exists.

Today, Bantams can still be seen in regular, daily use, particularly in the more rural areas. It will be a long time before this amazing little machine is confined to museums only, or to the many classic bike events that are run in most parts of the country throughout the year.

H.6942

CLUBS, SPECIALISTS & BOOKS

Clubs

There is no club that caters for BSA Bantam owners alone, unless the machine is to be used for racing. Under these circumstances membership of the **Bantam Racing Club** becomes an essential requirement, not only to be eligible to compete in club events, but also to have access to the detailed regulations that cover the specification of a racing machine. The address to contact is:

Mrs. J. Andrews,
Secretary, Bantam Racing Club,
6, Kipton Close,
Rothwell,
Northants,
NN14 2DR,
England.

For the ordinary road rider, the **BSA Owners Club** includes Bantam owners amongst its ranks and will prove helpful with regard to the regular interchange of information. In this instance, the address is:

Mr. D. Jones,
18, Round Wood Close,
Cyncoed,
Cardiff,
Glamorgan,
Wales.

Specialists

Reference to any of the more popular motorcycling magazines and newspapers will provide the names and addresses of many companies who specialise in Bantam spares, both new and second-hand. The magazines *Classic Bike* and *The Classic Motor Cycle* will prove particularly helpful in this respect.

Whilst it is always difficult to single out names and addresses, the following will make good starting points as acknowledged specialists in Bantam parts and sometimes literature:

Lewis and Sons (Weybridge) Ltd,
51, Church Street,
Weybridge,
Surrey, England.
(Weybridge 42210)

Martlesham Engineering Services,
15D, Gloster Road,
Martlesham Heath Airfield,
Ipswich,
Suffolk, England.
(0473 625207)

Harvey Owen,
181, Walworth Road,
London SE17, England.
(01-703 0282)

C & D Autos,
1193-1199, Warwick Road,
Acocks Green,
Birmingham B27 6BY, England.
(021-706 2902)

For many of the minor parts, including saddles, controls and electrical parts and fittings:

Armours,
784 Wimborne Road,
Bournemouth,
Hants, England.
(0384 55151)

Books

The main sources of literature relating to the BSA Bantam can be summarised as follows:

Original BSA Service Sheets and Bantam Handbook
May be available in original or reprinted form from any of the specialist suppliers listed previously. Good quality xerox copies are usually available from Bruce Main-Smith and Co., P.O. Box 20, Leatherhead, Surrey, England.

Pitmans Book of the BSA Bantam, by W.C. Haycraft. Five editions, from 1955 to 1966. All out-of-print but often obtainable at autojumbles and auctions.

BSA Bantam Owners Workshop Manual (No. 117). In print and available from Haynes Publishing Group, Sparkford, Yeovil, Somerset, England. Covers all models from 1948 to end of production.

BSA Gold Star and other Singles by Roy Bacon. In print and available from Osprey Publishing Ltd, 12-14, Long Acre, London, WC2E 9LB, England. Covers all BSA singles but has much useful data on Bantams including model identification and colour schemes.

Taking up Motor-Cycle Racing by Roy Bacon. Out-of-print, but often obtainable at autojumbles and auctions. Contains much useful data on preparing Bantams for racing, but was published in 1964 and is therefore dated.

Tuning for Speed by P.E. Irving. Out-of-print, but often obtainable at autojumbles and auctions, sometimes as a USA reprint. Third Edition (1956) contains data on tuning Bantam engines, now somewhat dated.

A Ride in the Sun by Peggy Iris Thomas. Out-of-print and not often found. First published in 1954 it is the account of a tour of Canada, the United States and Mexico by Peggy Thomas with her dog Matelot on the rear carrier of her D1 model. No illustrations.

Bantam Racing Club Tuning Manual. Available to Club members for £1.50. Non-members £2.50, from M.F.R. Baldwin, 9, Avondale Road, Leyton, London E17 8JG, England. Essential for all aspiring Bantam racers, as is club membership.

PHOTO GALLERY

1. This 1928 174cc BSA two-stroke is the ancestor of the BSA Bantam. The first two-stroke machine to be marketed by BSA Cycles Ltd, it proved a commercial failure and remained in production for only two years. Partially hidden behind the outside flywheel is the folding kickstarter. The object behind the engine unit is the toolbox, complete with lock (K. Harman)

2. Unusual features are the complete absence of a front brake (available as an optional extra) and the cross-over drive, with the kickstarter on the near side. The air cleaner can be seen pointing upwards, in line with the front downtubes of the frame. Found and restored by Ken Harman, a VMCC member living in Ashington, Sussex, the machine is in full running order. There is sone doubt as to whether the ML Maglita fitted behind the cylinder formed part of the original specification. (K. Harman)

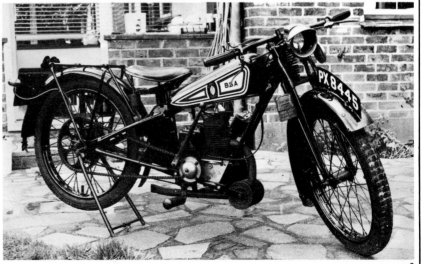

3

4

4A

3. The BSA Bantam was virtually a copy of the DKW RT125 model of the immediate pre-war era. The likeness is still evident in this photograph of a 1951 DKW RT125 model, apart from the transposition of the right and left-hand features of the engine unit. (Erwin Tragatsch)

4. One of the first Yamaha models, the YA1 of 1954, was also a copy of the DKW RT125. Only the unusual design of rear suspension and the cantilever saddle suggest other influences have been at work. (Motor Cycle Weekly)

4A. Harley-Davidson had their own version of the DKW RT125, catalogued originally as the 125cc 'Hummer'. This is the 1960 version, with an engine capacity increased to 165cc. It was designated the 'Super Ten'. (Harry V. Sucher)

Super Profile

5. Australian sheep farmers soon found a use for the BSA Bantam, this being one of the post-1955 150cc Bantam Major models fitted with swinging arm rear suspension. The sheep appears to be enjoying the ride! (Motorcycle Sport)

6. The Bushman model was the forerunner of the trail bike as we know it today. This photograph was taken at one of the provincial motorcycle shows, probably at Brighton during the mid-sixties. This is the D10 version of 173cc capacity. (Motorcycle Sport)

5

6

7

8

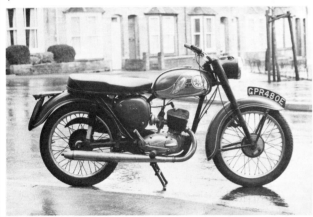

9

10

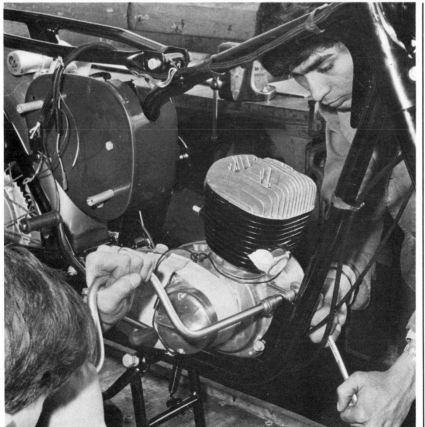

11

7. Some of the early D1 models proved invaluable in teaching learner riders to pass their driving test. This machine was used by Yeovil RAC/ACU Training Scheme and is in remarkably original condition.

8. As can be seen from the tax disc, this machine was still in constant use during 1976, after superficial restoration to the finish. Note the unusual, but sensible, method of mounting the bulb horn, this model having no battery.

9. This photograph of a D14/4 model was taken during 1973, outside the premises in Yeovil originally owned by Bryan Goss. A great many of these models were at the time still in daily use and this 1967 model was for sale in the showrooms.

10. Many impressive-looking trials 'specials' have been based on the BSA Bantam, and this is a particularly outstanding example. Machines such as this were capable of putting up a very creditable performance, in the right hands. (Motorcycle Sport)

11. This 'works' photograph shows a D14/4 engine unit being installed in a frame on the Bantam production line. (Cyril Halliburn)

12. A completed D14/4 goes out on road test, prior to delivery to a dealer. Note the protective tape across the front mudguard, to prevent the front fork legs from scuffing the paintwork. (Cyril Halliburn)

12

13

14

13. Final check point. The papers are signed before the machine is despatched from the works to the dealer who has placed the order. (Cyril Halliburn)

14. It was the Australians who first realised the potential of the BSA Bantam for road racing, when suitably tuned. One of the most famous was the Walsh Bantam, seen here being ridden by Don Cameron during March 1957. (Motorcycle Sport)

15. The spirit of Bantam racing. Mole Benn leads Fred Launchbury and Roy Bacon on lap 7 of the 4th race at Cadwell Park during August 1964. This is as far apart as the trio ever got! (Brian A. Holder)

15

16

17

18

19

16. Martin Baldwin and Brian Ing fight it out during a Bantam Racing Club event held during 1979. The photograph was taken at the Hairpin on the Lydden Circuit, Kent. (Brian Ing).

17. There's no limit to ingenuity! The 'Mighty Midget' racing car owned by J. Goss, of Adelaide, Australia, achieved some remarkable successes in hillclimb events. The 125cc D1 engine was tuned by Eric Walsh of Findlay Brothers, the BSA motorcycle distributors for Victoria. The car amazed everyone by ascending the Rob Roy hillclimb in 40 seconds, during the Australian Championships. (Ted Fithian)

18. This 1953 D1 model has been restored by Mr. J. Eyles, of Eastleigh, Hants. It is the, now somewhat rare, Lucas battery lighting model with coil ignition.

19. An off-side view of the same machine. It has the optional plunger-sprung frame and features the new design of silencer with detachable baffles.

20

21

22

23

20. The headlamp has an unusual shape of ammeter and a switch with the ignition key in the centre. The D-shaped speedometer was a popular fitment to many lightweight machines.

21. Not too clearly shown here, the headlamp had a

separate, underslung pilot light, which today would be of questionable legality. Note the mounting bracket, bolted to the fork lower yoke.

22. Although vacant on this machine, which has an electrically-operated horn, the centre of the steering head assembly was usually used to locate a downwards

pointing bulb horn on the direct lighting and competition models.

23. The rear lamp had this distinctive pattern plastic lens, retained by two screws. It will fracture easily if the screws are over-tightened.

24

25

26

27

28

24. The plunger-sprung rear suspension has only limited movement, but will take the worst jars out of pot holes. The sliders need to be greased regularly through the grease nipple provided. The rear wheel can be drawn backwards by means of the drawbolts on each side, to effect correct chain tension. Brake adjustment is carried out by turning the spring-loaded thumbwheel.

25. The early engines are characterised by the somewhat scanty finning of the cylinder head and barrel. Note the fins at the top of the crankcase casting.

26. A close-up of the redesigned silencer, which has detachable baffles to aid cleaning out the exhaust system at regular intervals. The rear mudguard stays are attached to the top bolt of the plunger suspension units.

27. How the front mudguard stays are attached to the front forks. The three mounting points are essential to prevent the mudguard from rotating if caught by the wheel.

28. The gear position indicator and pointer. This is a homemade version of the original, the correct transfer now being very difficult to obtain.

29

30

31

32

29. The rear carrier is an integral part of one set of mudguard stays and is a very useful fitting to have.

30. All rigid and plunger-sprung models are fitted with a three-point fixing saddle. This provides a surprisingly comfortable ride.

31. This 'bird's eye' view shows the layout of the controls and the shape of the early petrol tank. In those days, ball-ended levers were almost unknown.

32. A close-up of the distinctive petrol tank transfer. It is questionable whether this is an exact reproduction of the original, due to the different colour used for the wing on the BSA motif.

33. A quite small Amal carburettor of the 261 type was used on the D1 models. The detachable bell-mouth has strangler-type shutters, to aid cold starting.

34. The toolbox has the lid retained by a single Dzus fastener, operated by inserting a coin edge. The rectifier can just be seen, sandwiched between the toolbox and the battery. Originally, there was neither a hole nor a grommet in the toolbox top.

33

34

36

37

35

35. This smart-looking battery carrier is not exactly to original design, which did not carry a transfer either. This component is likely to corrode away quite easily from the effects of acid spray.

36. The D1 model fitted with Lucas battery lighting and coil ignition has a quite different type of left-hand crankcase cover compared to the Wico-Pacy direct lighting model.

37. The 1955 D3 model modified by the author into, basically, a competition model. The front mudguard has had its mounting changed by the present owner, Mr. P. Dungey of Milborne Port, Dorset, no doubt in an attempt to gain even better clearance.

38. The petrol tank is from a D1 model and does not carry the 'Bantam Major' motif. Braced motocross-type handlebars are fitted and the prop stand is from a BSA four-stroke.

38

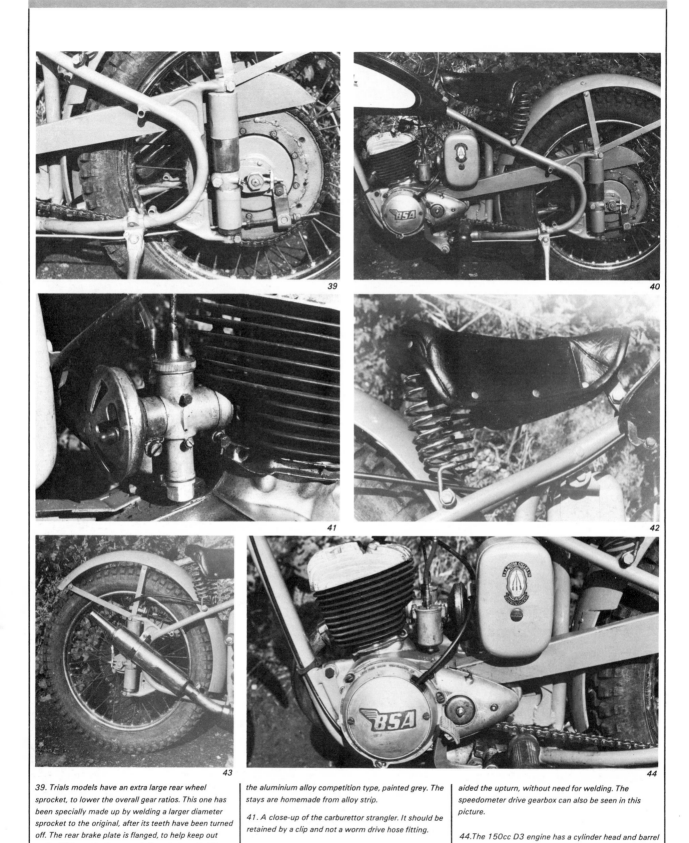

39

40

41

42

43

44

39. Trials models have an extra large rear wheel sprocket, to lower the overall gear ratios. This one has been specially made up by welding a larger diameter sprocket to the original, after its teeth have been turned off. The rear brake plate is flanged, to help keep out water. This rear brake seems to have lost most of its adjustment, which suggests the linings need renewing.

40. A close-up of the rear end. The mudguards are of the aluminium alloy competition type, painted grey. The stays are homemade from alloy strip.

41. A close-up of the carburettor strangler. It should be retained by a clip and not a worm drive hose fitting.

42. This replacement saddle, of the correct type, is a replica made by Armours, of Bournemouth.

43. The upswept, barrel-type silencer is not original, yet is quite effective. A very short length of flexible pipe has aided the upturn, without need for welding. The speedometer drive gearbox can also be seen in this picture.

44. The 150cc D3 engine has a cylinder head and barrel with much deeper fins. The rear brake pedal and footrests are not to original specification. The Wico-Pacy generator stator plate is retained by three screws. Slots permit the points assembly to be rotated within certain limits, to obtain accurate ignition timing.

45. The direct lighting model has the toolbox on the left, with a clip to retain the generator to sparking plug lead.

46. The 173cc D7 model has the word 'Super' cast on the left-hand crankcase cover. Despite its appearance, the original type of Wico-Pacy generator lies below, with its own separate cover as on the earlier models.

47. An unusual shot of the underside of a D7 model. The centre stand appears to be missing, hence the use of a non-standard prop stand.

48

49

50

51

52

53

48. Yet another design of silencer – the long 'torpedo' type with a fishtail end, fitted to the D7 model. In this shot, the detachable baffle assembly is evident from the protruding rod and nut.

49. A curved rear brake operating arm is used, to clear the end of the swinging arm fork. The D7 brake plate has a separate torque arm mounting.

50. The D7 engine has the deeper finned cylinder head and barrel, and is fitted with an Amal Monobloc carburettor with integral float chamber.

51. The hydraulically-damped front forks of the D7 model have detachable ends to aid wheel removal and revised single point mountings for the combined front and rear mudguard stays.

52. The D7 headlamp assembly contains a circular, magnetic-type speedometer, and a revised form of lighting switch. The speedometer is still of the non-trip type.

53. The D7 rear suspension units are both long and slim. The rear mudguard has side valances.

54

56

55

54. Yet another design of rear lamp lens. A stoplight is included in the specification of the D7 model.

55. This near-side view of an 'as found' D7 model, owned by Mr. D. Jenkin of Yeovil, Somerset, shows the greatly improved petrol tank with the 'starburst' BSA badge like that of the larger capacity BSA four-strokes.

Finish is in bright red, relieved by black and chrome plating.

56. The improved design of petrol tank fitted to the D7 model has chromium plated side panels that complement the brilliant red finish of this particular machine.

57

57. The offside of the same machine. The side panel has helped fill the ugly gap opposite the new shape toolbox, and the exhaust system is now of the long, tapering type.

58

59

60

61

58. *The D175 model is now somewhat rare, as it sold in comparatively small numbers. It can be identified by the central sparking plug, the gaitered front forks and exposed springs of the rear suspension units, and the 'jellymould' petrol tank. This machine too is owned by Mr. D. Jenkin of Yeovil, Somerset, and is of 1969 manufacture. It is in 'as found' condition.*

59. *A close-up of the D175 engine unit and the more shapely petrol tank, with yet another design of plastic tank badge. The central plug cylinder head of the D175 model has fins of different profile, compared to those of the earlier models.*

60. *An Amal type 626 Concentric carburettor was fitted to the D175 models. In this photograph, the air cleaner hose needs reconnecting and the control cables straightening.*

61. *Yet another method of mounting the front mudguard stays. The essential third location is made to a lug at the rear of each fork slider, higher up.*

62. *The headlamp of the D175 model is a separate unit, bolted to brackets on the fork upper shrouds. There are now two switches and an ignition warning light, as well as another design of magnetic speedometer calibrated up to 80mph.*

62

63. *The right-hand headlamp switch controls the lighting system. Beam height is adjusted by slackening the mounting bolts and tilting the headlamp shell according to requirements before retightening.*

64. *The D175 model has the electric horn on the right-hand side, to the rear of the side panel.*

65. *The D175 silencer has a more pronounced torpedo shape, the fishtail end having been abandoned. Detachable baffles are still a necessary requirement.*

66. *Although the front brake has remained on the right-hand side of the front wheel, it has its own torque arm.*

67. *A close-up of the circular plastic tank badge used on the D14/4 and D175 models. It is retained by two crosshead screws.*

68. *On the later 173cc models, the contact breaker assembly was transferred to the right-hand side of the machine. This necessitated a new design of crankcase outer cover, with a detachable inspection plate.*

69. *The left-hand crankcase outer cover had to be changed in profile too. The clutch adjustment hole is normally blanked off by a rubber plug.*

63

64

65

66

67

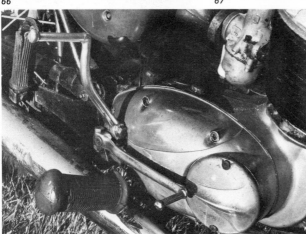

68

69

70

70. *The slim profile of the 'jellymould' tank is clearly seen from this position. The Concentric carburettor needs a separate handlebar-mounted air control for cold starting.*

71. *The more robust front forks fitted to the D175 model have gaiters in place of the previously-used long shrouds.*

72. *The rear brake stoplamp switch is clamped to the subframe tube and connected to the brake pedal by means of a long extension spring. Adjustment is effected by raising or lowering the switch.*

73. *The right-hand side of the D175 model showing the long, tapering exhaust system and the generally more sturdy appearance. Even so, it was no match for the Japanese lightweights that were flooding the UK market.*

71

72

73

C1

C1A

C2

C1. This is the pre-war DKW RT125, of which the BSA Bantam became a mirror copy. Rights to the design were acquired as the result of reparations to the allied forces when hostilities ended during 1945. This particular machine is now in the museum of VEB Motorradwerk Zschopau, the former DKW factory in East Germany. (VEB Motorradwerk Zschopau)

C1A. This 1953 model D1 Bantam, owned and restored by Mr. J.W. Eyles, has the optional plunger suspension frame and Lucas rectified current lighting. These two options would have added over £13 to the purchase price of the standard model.

C2. The right-hand side of the same machine, showing the ammeter mounted in the headlamp shell, in front of the light switch with its ignition key. The tubular silencer did not come into general use until 1954.

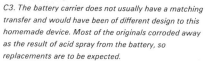

C3. The battery carrier does not usually have a matching transfer and would have been of different design to this homemade device. Most of the originals corroded away as the result of acid spray from the battery, so replacements are to be expected.

C4. The characteristic Bantam petrol tank transfer. The original design probably had the wing of the BSA motif in the same colour, and not in white.

C5. The toolbox lid carried the famous 'piled arms' motif that has long been associated with BSA. On earlier models, two Dzus fasteners were used.

C6. The original flat-type silencer is very difficult to find and does not have a long service life. The later, tubular type of silencer has the advantage of detachable baffles to make cleaning easier.

C7. All early engines can be identified by the shape of the cylinder head and barrel, small in area by later standards. It will be seen how the kickstarter and gearchange lever share a common axis.

C6

C7

C9

C8

C8. The lower ends of the front fork legs have lugs for the mounting of the mudguard stays. Note the method used to anchor the front brake plate.

C9. The 1955 D3 Competition Model restored by the author departs from the original specification in several respects but is very functional in use. The new owner has devised an alternative front mudguard mounting.

C10. The petrol tank is probably from a later D1 model, and has the correct 125 Bantam transfer. The 150cc models had the word 'Major' added to the transfer.

C10

C11. The 150cc engine has the benefit of deeper finning on both the cylinder barrel and head. The rear brake pedal and footrest mountings are not to the original specification. The external clutch adjuster is readily accessible, taking the form of a screw and locknut. Slots in the generator cover allow the stator to be rotated within certain limits for the correct ignition timing.

C12. The 175cc D7 Super Bantam broke new ground with a bright colour scheme and featured a more shapely petrol tank, mudguards and toolbox. By now, swinging arm rear suspension had superseded the earlier and less satisfactory plunger type. This is a 1960 standard model. Ignore the plastic 'stretch' seat cover!

C11

C12

C13

C13. A close-up of the swinging arm rear suspension and its long, slim suspension units. The toolbox has a much greater capacity, is more shapely, and fills in an unsightly gap. On this side a matching cover conceals the horn and rectifier.

C14. The original concept of the engine unit remains basically unchanged – and still there are only three gears. The right-hand crankcase cover has been cleaned up to present a more smooth profile.

C14

C15

C17

C15. Despite the use of a new left-hand crankcase cover bearing the name of the model, the original Wico-Pacy generator is housed within, with its own separate cover. In keeping with the times, an Amal Monobloc carburettor is used, with its own integral float chamber.

C16. The new petrol tank is of a much more pleasing shape and carries plastic tank badges similar to those used on the larger capacity BSA models. The chrome-plated side panels help to offset the brilliant red finish and add to the general appeal of this model.

C17 The strengthened telescopic forks have hydraulic damping and detachable ends to simplify front wheel removal. This has necessitated rearranging the method of attaching the front mudguard stays. The front brake is now $5\frac{1}{2}$ inches in diameter.

C16

Super Profile

C18

C18. The last in the line – the D175 Model identified by the centrally-located sparking plug, heavier front forks with separately-mounted headlamp, and rear suspension units with exposed springs. This is a 1969 model. Another plastic seat cover!

C19. The left-hand side of the same model. The petrol tank now has the 'jelly mould' shape, first introduced during 1965, with yet another design of plastic tank badge. By now, the contact breaker assembly has been transferred to the right-hand side of the machine, a change made when the D10 Supreme model was introduced during 1966.

C19

56